THE MAGIC:
EARVIN JOHNSON

THE MAGIC:
EARVIN JOHNSON

BILL MORGAN

SCHOLASTIC INC.
New York Toronto London Auckland Sydney

Photo Credits

ISBN 0-590-46050-1

12 11 10 9 8 7 6 5 4 3 2   2 3 4 5 6 7/9

Printed in the U.S.A.   40

First Scholastic printing, September 1992

Acknowledgments

The author gratefully acknowledges the staffs of the reference rooms at the Jefferson Market, Mid-Manhattan, and Main Branches of the New York Public Library; Dennis Swain and the following people at Scholastic: Jack Roberts, Nancy Farrell, Brook Kindred, Deborah Thompson, John Simko, and Nancy Smith; and, finally, thanks to my editor, Kate Waters.

This book is dedicated to everyone
who is working to educate us
about HIV and AIDS.

THE MAGIC:
EARVIN JOHNSON

Preface:
Magic Stuns the World

"**B**ecause of the HIV virus I have obtained, I will have to retire from the Lakers today."

With those words, spoken on November 7, 1991, Earvin "Magic" Johnson stunned the world. All across America, people stopped what they were doing when they heard the news about Magic.

All three television networks covered Magic's press conference live, and local stations broke away from regular programming to deliver the news.

In high school, college, and professional gyms and arenas, basketballs stopped bouncing as players heard the news that Magic had tested positive for HIV, the virus that causes AIDS.

As Magic spoke at the Great Western Forum, the home arena of his team, the Los Angeles

Lakers, he made it clear that, "Life is going to go on for me, and I'm going to be a happy man." Magic was determined to prove that being HIV positive did not mean he was going to quit living.

Magic was quick to add that his new wife, Cookie, was pregnant but that she and their unborn baby had both tested HIV negative. He also stated that he planned to play basketball for the U.S. Olympic team in Barcelona in June of 1992.

It was a surprising announcement from one of professional basketball's best players. For Magic, it was also a chance to begin educating Americans, especially young Americans, about HIV and AIDS.

"I think sometimes we think that, well, only gay people can get it, it's not going to happen to me," Johnson said at the press conference. "And here I am saying that it can happen to anybody. Even me, Magic Johnson."

What Magic was trying to do was spread the word that HIV and AIDS was everybody's disease. In the days that followed his announcement, teachers, parents, and kids talked about Magic, safer sex, and AIDS. AIDS clinics and hotlines across the country reported a record number of calls for information and requests for the HIV test. All of a sudden, everyone in America knew someone who was HIV positive.

For his teammates and his other friends in the NBA, it was a loss. In twelve seasons with the Lakers, Magic had led the team to five NBA titles. Fans in every city where the Lakers played loved the fast-paced style of Laker basketball, and especially number 32. Not only was Magic one of the NBA's best players, he was like a kid on the court, all smiles, high fives, and cheers when his team won a game.

It had been an incredible career for Magic. With his retirement, pro basketball lost one of its greatest players. But America was not losing one of its heroes.

As Magic ended his press conference, he looked at the reporters gathered in front of him, smiled, and left them with this message. "When your back is up against the wall, you have to come out swinging. I'm going to go on, going to be there, going to have fun."

Magic did just that. Three months after his announcement, Magic was back at the NBA All-Star Game in Orlando.

1
The Kid
with the Basketball

Imagine that there is this kid in your neighborhood and, every time you see him, he has a basketball. Sometimes he is just walking down the street dribbling that ball. Other times, he is on his bicycle, one hand gripping the handlebars, while the other bounces the ball as he pedals. And still other times, he is carrying a bag of groceries in one arm, the other arm in constant motion, bouncing and bouncing that basketball.

The people who lived in Lansing, Michigan, during the late 1960's and early 1970's didn't have to use their imagination. They would watch a certain kid from the neighborhood, always bouncing a basketball, and say, "There goes Junior."

Junior was Earvin Johnson, Jr. In high school

he would be given the nickname Magic, but as a youngster bouncing a basketball through the streets of Lansing, he was simply known as Junior.

Earvin Johnson, Jr., was born on August 14, 1959, to Earvin and Christine Johnson. Earvin, Sr., and Christine had met while he was in the service. They married and moved to Lansing and immediately became a family. Earvin senior already had three children, and they now lived with their father and his new wife. Earvin was the third child born to Earvin senior and Christine. After Earvin junior was born in 1959, the Johnsons had four more children.

Junior and the rest of the Johnson children grew up in a yellow frame house on Middle Street in Lansing. A mid-size town located about ninety miles northwest of Detroit, Lansing is the state capital of Michigan. It is a working-class town full of automobile plants, construction industries, and government offices.

Middle Street was, not surprisingly, in the middle of Lansing in a lower-middle-class neighborhood. There were lots of kids in the neighborhood. The streets were safe enough to play in, and games, and later sports, kept many kids busy and out of trouble.

Inside the house on Middle Street, Christine made sure the kids helped around the house and that the normal fights between brothers and sisters remained under control. Earvin senior often worked three jobs, so he was seldom home.

From an early age, the Johnson children saw how hard their father worked. They behaved so that, when their father came home from a long day and night of work, he had no reason to be angry with them.

Earvin senior worked long hours to make sure his family had food, clothing, and shelter. His day started at an automobile plant where he worked the 5 P.M. to 1 A.M. shift on an assembly line. After leaving the plant, Earvin would sometimes do odd jobs for some of the local businesses in Lansing. One he did often (and one that Junior helped him with when he got older) was to soap down and scrub the oil-stained floors of mechanic shops and gas stations.

Arriving home in the middle of the night, Earvin senior would get a few hours sleep. Then he would wake up, get in his truck, and haul rubbish. By noon, he was ready for another few hours of sleep before getting up in the late afternoon to report to the assembly line at the automobile plant to begin a new day.

From the beginning, Junior and the rest of the Johnson children were taught that if they wanted something, they had to work for it. It was no surprise, therefore, that Junior would soon be a hard-working member of the family. Junior was often seen mowing neighborhood lawns in the summer and shoveling snow from his neighbors' sidewalks in the winter. By the time he was ten, Junior had his own lawn-mowing business with his own lawn mower.

But it wasn't all work. After all, he was still pretty young when he was seen bouncing that basketball all over town.

As much as Junior loved his family, when he got a little older he wanted some privacy. *And* some peace and quiet. Ten children can create quite a bit of noise, whether it's good-natured teasing, babies crying, or just constant noise created by so many people.

Junior found that a basketball and the backboard set up in the family driveway gave him some time to himself. He began to spend his free time bouncing the ball and trying, without much success, to toss the ball into the basket that towered over him. At first it was almost comical, this short kid trying time after time to get the big orange ball in the net. But Junior continued to throw the ball toward the net until finally, one day, he made a basket.

His father noticed Junior's interest in basketball and decided to encourage his son to play. Earvin senior had played basketball as a kid and was a real fan of the game. He watched the Detroit Pistons on television whenever he could.

It was in front of the television that Junior began to learn the game. Earvin senior would explain everything about the game to his son — from the fundamentals of dribbling to the finer points of setting up an offensive play.

Earvin senior told his son to watch the players when they dribbled the basketball. They didn't watch the ball; they were able to dribble the ball and keep their heads up. This enabled them to watch their teammates, and their opponents, to see if someone was coming at them to steal the ball or block a pass. Earvin senior also taught his son the importance of watching the whole court and not just the man with the ball. He explained the different positions: how the guards brought the ball up the court and set up the offensive plays, how the forwards and the center tried to position themselves close to the basket. Junior listened to his father and watched the Pistons do what his father was explaining.

What Earvin senior was trying to teach his son from the very beginning was that basketball requires a team effort. It takes more than one man to make a basket and score two points. It takes a team. Every player has a role in helping the team win, from the guard controlling the offensive flow of the game to the center positioning himself for an offensive rebound.

From those early lessons in front of the television, Junior liked the idea of being a guard — the guy who controlled the game and set up the offensive plays.

After the Piston games on television were over, father and son went out to the driveway. There, Earvin senior taught his son to apply the techniques he had just seen on television. The two Earvins spent hours working on dribbling, passing, rebounding, and shooting.

From the beginning, Junior loved the game

and spent hours practicing by himself. "Maybe I just didn't have any distractions. No beach, not a lot of expensive toys. Just sports," he remembered of those first days in the driveway.

Soon, he was bouncing and dribbling a basketball everywhere he went. The only place, besides the classroom, he wasn't allowed to dribble the ball was in the house. But that didn't stop him from practicing when it was raining outside and he couldn't play in the driveway. On those days, Junior would roll up some socks, get a pan from the kitchen and play imaginary basketball games by himself.

The sound of Junior dribbling a basketball soon became familiar to the Johnson family and their neighbors on Middle Street. Nobody minded the sharp slapping sound the ball made when Junior bounced the ball in the driveway. Or the smacking sound the ball made against the backboard. The neighbors did complain, however, when he bounced the ball on the wooden front porch of the Johnson home when snow covered the driveway. The dull thuds that echoed as the ball hit the wood were too much and, after twice using the porch as a substitute basketball court, Junior was ordered never to do it again.

His solution was to grab the snow shovel and, with basketball in hand, go to the local elementary school. There, one could hear the long scraping sounds of snow being shoveled off cement. These were soon replaced by the familiar ping of a basketball hitting cement. Nothing as minor as a snowstorm was going to stop Junior from playing basketball!

By the time he was in the fourth grade, Junior was playing in a few local recreational leagues around Lansing. Nearly every day he was in some gymnasium playing basketball. Even on Sundays, Junior would rush home from church, take off his Sunday suit, and put on the one suit he really felt comfortable in — his basketball uniform. On days when there wasn't a league game, Junior grabbed his basketball, dribbled it to a local park, and found some guys for a pick-up game.

It was at one of the local parks that Junior met another kid who loved basketball. His name was Jay Vincent. Jay and Junior were the same age and had equal basketball abilities. Junior went to the Main Street Elementary School and Jay went to the Holmes Street School. The two quickly became friends. Through the years, the two would play on different teams in Lansing and they later became friendly rivals in playground and school-sponsored games.

At the local playgrounds and parks, Junior would try to get in a game with older and taller kids. Even at an early age, he tried to challenge himself against better players. It wasn't too long before the older kids welcomed Junior on their teams because he could dribble between his legs and pass the ball behind his back. The older kids liked the way Junior played for another reason.

He wasn't like most players his age, hogging the ball and trying to take all the shots. Junior actually liked to pass the ball to his teammates. From an early age, Junior liked to make assists, passing the ball to a player so that he could make a basket.

Between the recreational leagues, and the pick-up games, Junior was improving his game. He was also developing skills that would make him a great all-around player. While many players excel at shooting, or dribbling, or passing, Junior was becoming good at all three. He was indeed becoming a *magical* young basketball player.

While Junior played in recreational leagues and playground pick-up games, the lessons in the driveway continued. As Junior grew taller and became more confident of his ability with a basketball, he felt that he was becoming a better player than his father. After all, he was younger than his father, played on a regular basis, and was about the same height. The only thing Junior didn't count on was the fact that his father was still smarter.

"I was really cocky. I thought I could go out there and beat up the old man. But he knew all the old tricks, like holding me with one arm and shooting with the other. Boy, he beat me. Something like 15–5. That brought me back to earth. That made me start to think the game — not just play it," remembered Junior years later.

Earvin senior was not through teaching his

11

son about basketball. Once Junior was comfortable using his right hand for dribbling, passing, and shooting, his father taught him another very valuable lesson. Earvin senior made Junior start doing everything with his left hand, too. He stressed that, if Junior only played using his right side, he was only playing with half of his body and using only half of his potential ability. There was no reason, he said, why a player shouldn't be able to fake a move to the left as much as to the right. If a player always fakes to the right, the opposing team is always going to know the direction of your movements. Junior saw the logic and began to work on using the left side of his body.

Junior would practice dribbling, passing, and shooting for hours using only his left hand. In the playground games, he would experiment using his left hand. He would dribble, pass to his teammates, and shoot the basketball with his left hand. It wasn't long before Junior saw just how important using the left hand would become.

In the fall of 1971, Junior entered the seventh grade at Dwight Rich Junior High in Lansing. Seventh graders were allowed to try out for the school basketball team. Junior could hardly wait.

2
Junior in Junior High

Imagine that you are going to your first school basketball tryout. It is your first chance to wear your school colors and play in front of your classmates. Now, imagine that you run down to the gym, open the door, and see two hundred other guys there. All waiting to try out for the team.

That was what awaited Junior when he arrived at the Dwight Rich Junior High School gym for basketball tryouts. Junior knew he was good, but he had never tried out for a team before. And there were so many other players.

The coach called all the players together and told them that their first requirement would be to make a lay-up. Everyone smiled. A lay-up is the easiest shot to make. But the coach had all the right-handed players line up on the left side of the court and all the left-handed players line up on the right-hand side of the court. Then he gave the basketball hopefuls the bad news.

To survive the first cut of the team, all right-handed players had to make the lay-up from the left side using their left hand. And the left-handed players had to make the lay-up from the right side using their right hand. Anyone who missed their first lay-up would be cut from the team. Immediately. The smiles soon faded. Except for one. The smile, that would years later become world famous, stayed on Junior's face.

Junior was one of twenty-five players to make that first cut. And he made all the other cuts and became a member of the Dwight Rich Junior High basketball team. Right after the tryout he ran home with the good news. And he thanked his father for making him learn to use his left hand.

In the coming years, there were more lessons to learn. It was soon evident that Junior was the best player on the team and it became easy for him to dominate the game. He would be all over the court; getting rebounds, dribbling the ball the length of the court, and making the basket. In some games he scored all but two or four of his team's points.

His teammates didn't mind. The team was winning every game. But the parents of the other players were not as happy. They hadn't come to a game to see someone else's kid hog the ball and score all the points. They wanted to see their own sons play. Or at least touch the ball once in a while.

The parents would start screaming for the coach to "take that Johnson kid out" so their kids could play. It wasn't easy for Junior to listen to their shouts from the bleachers. After all, he was only doing what came naturally to him — playing basketball to the best of his ability. He soon realized that he would have to change the way he was playing. Junior and his coach had a heart-to-heart talk and Junior promised to share the ball more with his teammates. It was an important moment in the young player's basketball life. He saw that his team kept winning and more of his teammates were helping the team to victory. And, at the same time, Junior was improving other aspects of his game. Especially his ability to pass the ball to his teammates. Everyone was happy. Especially the parents of his teammates.

While Junior was a student at Dwight Rich Junior High he met someone who became like a second father to him. Dr. Charles Tucker was the psychologist for the Lansing school district. One day he went to Junior's school to talk to the ninth graders about their roles and responsibilities in society.

After his speech, Dr. Tucker took off his coat and tie, put on his sweatpants and sneakers, and headed for the basketball court in the playground. Dr. Tucker had been a professional basketball player for a short time after graduating from Western Michigan University and he never missed an opportunity to shoot some hoops when he visited a school.

It was on that court that he met Junior. Dr. Tucker immediately saw that Junior was a gifted basketball player. Dr. Tucker challenged Junior to a game of one-on-one and soon Junior saw that his opponent was the most formidable player he had ever played against.

Junior quickly began to question his opponent about his defensive moves and other aspects of Dr. Tucker's game. Dr. Tucker promised to teach Junior what he knew, and the lessons began the very next day. Dr. Tucker became a friend, adviser, and coach to Junior.

It was also while Junior was in junior high that he met two other people that would change his life. In addition to loving the game of basketball, Junior began to develop an interest in the business world.

Part of that, no doubt, came from watching his father work so hard and running his own neighborhood lawn-mowing business at ten years of age. Junior's interest in business increased after he met and became friends with two local businessmen.

Joel Ferguson and Gregory Eaton were successful businessmen in Lansing. They were interested in the community in general, and kids in particular. Ferguson had a local basketball court paved and soon met Earvin Johnson, Jr. He was impressed immediately with Junior's talents with a basketball. But he was also impressed with Junior's determination to work hard at everything he did. It wasn't long before Junior was working for the two men.

One of the businesses the two men owned was a local dairy. Every day after school, when there wasn't basketball practice, Junior arrived, basketball in hand, and helped stack milk and other dairy products in the stockroom. He also delivered ginger ale for another company the businessmen ran.

Another job Junior had was as a janitor in an office building the two men owned. On Friday nights, after the office workers left, Junior would go into the building and clean. He would empty wastebaskets, vacuum the carpeting, and clean the rest rooms. When he finished his work, Junior would begin to daydream.

"I'd sit back in one of those chairs and put my feet up on the desk, and start giving orders to my staff. Do this, do that." And, as he would dream, he would think about what it would be like to be a successful businessman and a professional basketball player.

During the school year, Junior juggled basketball practice, schoolwork, and after-school jobs. In the summer he only had to juggle his jobs and his basketball practice. But there were a lot of basketball practices. As Junior got older, his love of the game didn't change. He continued to play basketball as much as he could.

As high school approached, Junior looked forward to playing for Sexton High. His playground buddy, Jay Vincent, would be on the team, too. But then the Johnson family learned that the school district was continuing to bus students from the Middle Street area to Everett High School in an almost all-white neighborhood.

No one in the Johnson household was happy with the decision. Junior wanted to go to Sexton with Jay and the rest of his friends. His parents wanted him to go to Sexton, too.

Junior's older brothers, Quincy and Larry, had gone to Everett and had not been happy there. Forced bussing of students had started when Quincy was at Everett and there had been some ugly racial incidents.

The racial incidents were over by the time Larry became a student at Everett but he had been unhappy at the school for another reason. The coach at Everett, George Fox, had cut Larry from the basketball team.

If Junior wasn't feeling too good about going to Everett, Coach Fox couldn't wait to get Junior on his team. Coach Fox had seen Junior playing in a Boy's Club league game the summer before he entered Everett. As he sat in the bleachers watching Junior play, he knew he was watching a kid with something special. Basketball at Everett High was about to change — for the better.

3
Junior Becomes Magic

Imagine you are entering high school and everybody knows that you are some hotshot basketball player. People from all over town have seen you play in recreational leagues and on the junior high team. The high school you are playing for had an unimpressive 11 wins and 12 losses last season. You may only be a sophomore, but everyone is counting on you to make the team a winner. A big winner.

That is how Junior entered Everett High School in the fall of 1974. "We knew we had a good player coming in," remembered George Fox. Junior *was* good. In fact, he was too good.

When basketball practice started, the other players on the Everett High team began to resent Junior's talent. He was able to grab a rebound, take the ball the length of the court, and make a basket without involving any of his teammates.

It wasn't long before the other members of the team kept the ball from Junior any time they got their hands on it. They just wouldn't pass to him, even if he was open under the basket. The situation got ugly and Junior got into a shouting match with one of the seniors. This was a new problem for Coach Fox and he tended to side with the older players. That made Junior furious. He threatened to quit the team.

Dr. Tucker talked to Junior and explained it was difficult for the older players to be upstaged by a sophomore. Junior was a better player and it was hard for the others to accept that fact.

Junior stayed with the team and, after Coach Fox changed his coaching style to take advantage of Junior's ability to throw a full-court pass or a no-look pass, the team began to come together. It was a good thing, too, because the basketball season was ready to begin.

There was a lot of pressure for Junior to perform well on the basketball court. But in his first game for the Everett High School Vikings, he didn't play very well. He certainly didn't look like a star of the future.

The bigger and tougher players from the other team intimidated Junior. He was afraid to shoot and, although the Vikings won, he didn't play a very good game. That was about to change.

In his second game, Junior gained confidence and played up to his ability. And he got better with each game.

It was during his first year at Everett High that Junior was given a nickname that, one day, would be known by the whole world. He was given that name one Friday afternoon after a game in which Junior had scored 36 points, grabbed 18 rebounds, made 16 assists, and stole the ball from the opposing team 20 times.

A local sportswriter from the *Lansing State Journal* named Fred Stabley, Jr., was watching that game. He couldn't believe his eyes. He had never seen a high school player, much less a sophomore, play such an incredible game of basketball. He decided right then and there that this kid needed a name other than Earvin or Junior.

In the locker room after the game, Stabley approached Junior and complimented him on his game. He told the youngster that he needed a nickname. Junior shrugged and smiled. Stabley's first choice was no good. He wanted to call Earvin, Jr., "Big E." The only problem was that Elvin Hayes of the Houston Rockets in the NBA already had that name. Stabley's second choice was no better. He wanted to call Junior, "Dr. J." The trouble was, Julius Erving of the Philadelphia 76ers already had that name.

Stabley thought in silence for a few more minutes about the game he had just watched. One word came to his mind to describe Junior's playing ability: magic. "That's it!" yelled Stabley. "We'll call you Magic."

"That's okay by me," replied Junior, not giving

it much thought at the time. And so, on a cold winter afternoon in a high school locker room smelling of dirty sneakers, a young kid who started throwing balls at a basket in a driveway, went from being Junior to nothing less than Magic.

And the magic continued for the rest of Junior's sophomore year. By the end of the season, the youngster, now known as Magic, led the Everett High Vikings in scoring, rebounds, and assists. The team went to the state basketball tournament and got as far as the quarterfinals. There they lost a heartbreaker to Dearborn Fordson High. Everett was winning the game by 13 points in the fourth quarter but let it slip away.

The team finished with a record of 22 wins and 2 losses. Magic became the first tenth-grader to be named to the All-State Team.

Even though the season had ended at Everett, basketball didn't end for Magic. He continued to play every chance he could get. Even on summer vacations.

The Johnson family went to visit relatives in North Carolina and soon Magic was at the local playground getting into games with local players.

They saw that Magic was a pretty good player. It wasn't long before he was challenged to a game of one-on-one. A small wager was attached to the game to make it more interesting. That turned out to be the only interesting thing about the challenge. Magic outplayed his challenger, beating him fifteen baskets to eight. The challenger asked his friends to lend him some money so he could play Magic again. They refused. They knew that on their local basketball court, they had indeed been witness to a magic show.

Back in Lansing, Magic went to an outdoor concert one summer evening. Also at the concert was his buddy from the playground days, Jay Vincent. They started to talk about basketball and, when intermission came, the two basketball talents headed to a nearby court. A two-on-two game was in progress featuring some ex-high-school stars of the area who had graduated a few years earlier. The winning team challenged Magic and Jay.

It was the last time Magic and Jay would play as a team in a playground game. They so thoroughly whipped the older players that word spread through the playgrounds of Lansing and no one else would play them.

Magic also went to the arena where the Michigan State University players practiced during the off-season. There he met Terry Furlow who later played in the NBA. Soon the two were going at it in one-on-one games. Magic couldn't beat the college star, but he could learn more about the game. And he did just that.

When the summer ended and it was time to go back to school, Magic was ready for his junior year on the Everett High basketball team.

The 1975–1976 basketball season went pretty

much the same for Everett High as the previous season. The team had an incredible 21–1 record after the regular season. In one game, Magic scored 54 points, breaking a city record for points in one game. He was named to the All-State Team for the second year in a row. He was also named the United Press International Prep School Player of the Year.

And, going into the state basketball tournament, Everett High was the number-one ranked team in the state. Everyone at Everett thought the team had a good chance of being state champions.

Magic wanted Everett to win the championship for his best friend on the team, Reggie Chastine. The two had become friends during Magic's sophomore year despite the fact that Magic was now six-and-a-half feet tall and Reggie was only five feet three inches. They both liked a fast-paced style of basketball, and Reggie played the other guard position. Reggie was a year older than Magic. It would be his last chance to be on a championship team.

But, as happens in sports, the number-one team doesn't always win the championship. In the semifinals, Everett lost in an upset to a team that wasn't even ranked in the Top Ten. It was a crushing blow to the team. And to Magic. Reggie graduated without playing on a championship team.

Then, tragedy struck.

During the summer of 1976, before Magic's

senior year, Reggie was killed in an automobile accident. It shocked the whole school. When the basketball team gathered for their first practice that fall, the team dedicated the season to Reggie and vowed to win the state championship in his honor.

As practices began for Magic's senior year at Everett, he was aware that he was becoming a famous basketball player throughout the state of Michigan. For awhile he let everything that was being said and written about him go to his head.

When practices started in the fall of his senior year, Magic began to slack off. He was bored with drills and didn't feel his talents were being challenged. He tried to see what he could get away with and he didn't practice with 100-percent effort. That didn't last long. After a couple of practices, Coach Fox pulled the youngster aside and whispered in his ear, "If you have the same attitude when you show up for practice tomorrow, you will start the next game on the bench."

Suddenly, Magic was Junior again. A kid that still had things to learn about the game of basketball. He looks back on this incident as his "wake-up call" and he didn't need to hear it twice.

Magic dedicated himself to being the best player, whether in practice or during a game. And to lead his team, by his ability *and* his attitude. He wanted to be known as a team player.

And he was determined to lead the Vikings to the state championship.

In fact, in the first few games of the season, he was almost too determined. Magic became the kind of player he had been before, trying to do everything to insure victory instead of being a team player. Everett High began to rack up victories and Magic was averaging about 40 points a game. Again, the team was winning but it was beginning to look like the Everett High Magic Team instead of the Everett High Vikings.

Coach Fox once again pulled his young superstar aside. Patiently, he explained that the team would do better if Magic scored less and played the all-around basketball game he was so good at. Coach Fox reminded Magic that basketball was a team game and that only the team could win the state championship. If Magic thought he could do it alone, he was sadly mistaken.

The words sunk in and in his next game, Magic went from scoring 40 points to scoring 12. But he made important assists and helped his team to another victory.

There would be many victories for the Vikings that year. The team lost only one game during the regular season.

And while basketball dominated Magic's life during the season, Junior was still a student and a member of the Johnson family.

He was the managing editor of the school newspaper and volunteered at the local Boy's

Club. At home, where he was still called Junior, he was still expected to work.

Every Saturday at 7 A.M. his father would wake Junior from a sound sleep. After asking how the team had done the night before, Earvin senior made sure his son got up and got ready to help haul rubbish. Earvin senior still had his hauling business and Junior helped him every Saturday — even during basketball season. And Junior did it without protest. For no matter how hard he worked at basketball, in school, or in the odd jobs he did to earn money, Junior knew that he never worked as hard as his father. It is a memory that has never left him.

Junior applied that same hard-work attitude to basketball. He was the first to show up for practice and the last to leave. He knew there was always some aspect of his game that he could work on and improve. Whether it was before high school practice or before a playground game, Magic would show up about 30 minutes ahead of schedule and do suicide drills. Suicide drills are designed to build up stamina so a player doesn't get winded while running up and down the court during practice or a game.

Beginning at one end of the court, Magic would sprint to the nearest foul line and back to the edge of the court. Then he would run at full speed to the line at the middle of the court and back. Then Magic would run to the opposite free-throw line and back to the starting point, again running full-out. Finally, he would sprint the length of the court and back. After a 30-second break, he would do it all over again . . . five times. By the time practice started, Magic was warmed up and ready to go. And during practice, or in a game, as the other players began to tire, Magic wasn't running out of breath. His teammates constantly asked him how he kept in shape. It was one secret he kept to himself.

After practice, Magic remained in the gym and worked on different aspects of his game. Sometimes he would just lie on the floor and dribble the basketball hundreds of times next to his body. Just dribble and dribble the ball so he could get even more familiar with the way it felt against his fingertips. It was a good way to wind down after practice while still doing something that helped improve his game.

His hard work and dedication paid off. In March of 1977, the Everett High School Vikings made it to the state basketball final at the Crisler Arena on the campus of the University of Michigan in Ann Arbor. More than 13,000 fans jammed the arena to see the game between Everett and Brother Rice.

It was a hard fought game. Neither team could build up a big lead. Magic played a great game but fouled out with more than a minute to play. When Magic fouled out, the Vikings had a precious five-point lead. As Magic sat on the bench watching his teammates play without him, the words of Coach Fox entered his head. The coach had been right. If Magic had been allowed to dominate the Vikings' games, his teammates would not have had the ability to hold on to the lead. But they did. And the Everett High School Vikings won the game 62–56 to become the 1977 high school basketball champions in the state of Michigan.

It was a sweet victory. It had been a team effort and the Vikings had kept their promise to win the state championship for their ex-teammate Reggie. For Magic, it was a terrific way to end his high school basketball career. Once again, Magic was named to the All-State Team, the first player ever to be named three years in a row.

But most importantly, Magic had learned a lesson he would never forget. Basketball was a team game. And, as nice as all the awards and all the newspaper articles about him were, they wouldn't have meant anything if the team hadn't won that game.

4
From State Champ to National Champ

Imagine that it is time to choose a college. Many schools want you to play for their basketball team. Scouts and coaches call you on the telephone and come knocking at your door. There isn't a moment of peace. Do you go with the school that is already known as a basketball powerhouse? Or do you go with the university that could use a little magic on the court?

In the spring and summer of 1977, after Everett High won the state basketball championship in Michigan, that was the question facing Magic.

Both the University of Michigan in Ann Arbor and Michigan State University in East Lansing were anxious for Magic to remain in his home state and help their schools to basketball glory.

Colleges and universities all over the country

were trying to convince Magic to join their teams. Coaches and scouts from such schools as Notre Dame, the University of Maryland, the University of North Carolina, and UCLA were doing their best to recruit Magic.

The National Collegiate Athletic Association (NCAA) rules allow a potential basketball scholarship student to visit six schools while trying to make a decision. Magic visited only four. He traveled to Maryland, the University of Michigan, Notre Dame, and the University of North Carolina. He didn't go to UCLA because the university canceled his trip as another potential basketball star was scheduled to visit the same weekend and they didn't want both potential scholarship students on campus at the same time. When Magic held firm, saying he would either visit on the scheduled weekend or would never visit, UCLA claimed they couldn't host the Michigan star. Magic crossed UCLA off his list of possible schools.

He also didn't visit Michigan State. The university was located in nearby East Lansing and Magic knew the campus and was friends with some of the players on the team.

After a lot of discussions and visits to the schools, Magic narrowed his choice to between Michigan State University and the University of Michigan.

It was a tough choice for the seventeen-year-old high school star. The University of Michigan had a strong basketball program and often played on national television. Michigan State wasn't known for its basketball program. While Magic and the Everett Vikings were winning the 1977 high school championship, the Michigan State Spartans had won only ten games while losing seventeen.

The University of Michigan seemed the logical choice. And then, Magic spoke to his father and to his friend, Dr. Charles Tucker.

Since Michigan State was in nearby East Lansing, Earvin senior strongly urged his son to go there. While Dr. Tucker agreed that the University of Michigan had a better team, he pointed out that Magic could help turn the Spartans into a winner and that the school in East Lansing already had some good players. Magic decided to attend Michigan State.

"I like the underdog school," said Magic when he announced he had chosen Michigan State. "Every team I've played on was not supposed to win. Even when I go to the playground I don't pick the best players, I pick the players who want to work hard."

Magic entered Michigan State in the fall of 1977 and, although home was nearby, he chose to live in a dorm on campus. His roommate was none other than his old playground friend and rival, Jay Vincent. Jay had also chosen Michigan State, so the two players who had torn up playground basketball courts were reunited and hoping to tear up the NCAA with their teamwork.

As soon as Magic entered Michigan State he became a favorite on the East Lansing campus. His smile and friendly personality made him an instant hit. He chose telecommunications as a major and hoped one day to be a television announcer after his basketball playing days were over. From the beginning, Magic studied hard and took the academic side of college life very seriously.

Basketball practice began soon after Magic and Jay started their freshman year. Both worked hard to become starting players for the Spartans. Unlike the first days at Everett High, there wasn't a problem with the older players on the Michigan State team.

Greg Kesler, a junior, was the best-known player on the team and he played the forward position. Bob Chapman, another returning player, started as the other guard. The two veterans and the two freshmen were to be the core of the new Spartan basketball team, and everyone on campus looked forward to their first game against Western Michigan.

While Magic didn't experience the same rough times in early practices with the Spartans as he had in high school, he did play a lackluster first game. And again it was due to nerves.

In his collegiate debut, Magic only scored 7 points. Jay Vincent, on the other hand, was magnificent, scoring 25 points and leading the Spartans to a come-from-behind win over Western Michigan.

Then, just as he had done at Everett High, Magic began to feel more confident in his second game, and he began to play better. Soon he was the star of the Spartan team. But not because he was scoring all the points. Spartan Coach Judd Heathcote used Magic wisely. And his teammates quickly found out that if they could break for the basket while Magic had the ball, he would pass it to them as they leaped in the air. From there it was a lay-up or a dunk for another easy Spartan basket.

The Spartans rolled to a 12–1 record early in their freshman season against nonconference teams. As they began to play their Big Ten conference opponents, the Spartan fans had visions of their first Big Ten title since 1959.

The Spartans did not disappoint. Magic, Jay, and Greg Kesler led Michigan State to a 15–3 Big Ten record and won the conference championship. That meant an automatic bid to the NCAA College Basketball Championship Tournament.

The Spartans defeated their first two opponents, Providence and Western Kentucky, to reach the Mideast Regional final. They faced the number one team in the nation, the University of Kentucky.

The game started with Michigan State playing a fast and furious brand of basketball to pull ahead early against Kentucky. At the half, the Spartans led by five points.

In the second half, for some reason, Coach

Heathcote slowed down the pace of the game. That was more to the liking of the Kentucky Wildcats and they were able to catch the Spartans and move ahead. At the final buzzer, the Wildcats emerged as winners and eventually went on to win the national championship.

It was a tough loss for the Spartans who felt they could have won. Coach Heathcote took the blame for slowing down the pace of the game. But, overall, it had been a successful year for the Spartans, and especially for Magic.

And in typical Magic style, he wasn't just piling up impressive statistics. In fact, on paper, he didn't appear to be a great player. During his freshman year he averaged only 7 assists per game and 17 points. But what the statistics didn't show was Magic's influence on the court and his special ability to lead the Spartans to victory.

"In Earvin's case you don't talk about the points he produces," said Coach Heathcote after Magic's freshman year. "Not just the baskets and assists, but the first pass that makes the second pass possible."

In typical Magic style, he knew how to find the man who would be able to pass to the man under the basket who would then make the basket. That move doesn't show up in the statistics. But knowledgeable fans, coaches, and professional scouts could easily appreciate Magic's unselfish style of play.

Magic had come a long way from dominating

a game to controlling it. As the guard, he would bring the ball up court and set up his team's offensive strategy. Like his father had taught him in front of the television, Magic was able to see the whole court as he set up the Spartan offense. He could see which of his teammates were open while anticipating his opponent's next move.

"His court vision is fantastic," said Coach Heathcote of his star player's ability to see the entire court.

"My whole game is court sense," Magic said after his freshman season. "Being smart, taking charge, setting up a play, or, if I have to, scoring."

As the college scouts had watched Magic play in high school, the professional scouts now watched his college games. Soon after Michigan State lost in the tournament, Magic got an offer to leave school and join a professional team.

The Kansas City Kings offered Magic a $1.5-million contract to join their team. At eighteen, Magic was being asked to make a major decision concerning his future. Luckily, there were family and friends around to advise the youngster.

After much discussion and some meetings with the Kansas City Kings, Magic said no. As tempting as the money was, Magic liked campus life and wanted to be part of an NCAA championship team.

A sigh of relief sounded on the Michigan State campus when it was announced that he would return for his sophomore year. But before he did, there was more basketball to play in the summer of 1978. Magic went to Europe with a team of college all-stars to play some exhibition games.

One of his teammates on that all-star squad was a sandy-haired kid from Indiana named Larry Bird. It was the only time these two future superstars played on the same team. Unknown to both players, they would be on opposing teams the next March, playing for the national collegiate championship.

It was also during the summer before his sophomore year that Earvin Johnson became known as "EJ the DJ." Two nights a week, he worked as a disc jockey at a disco in East Lansing called Bonnie and Clyde's. EJ the DJ soon found that he liked controlling the dancers as much as he liked controlling a game of basketball.

"The fun part was that I could make 'em dance or sit down. It was up to me whether they were going to go home early or stay all night."

Another important non-basketball event happened to Magic while he was at Michigan State. He met a girl named Earletha Kelly. The two began dating. They would continue to date, off and on, for the next twelve years before getting married.

As the summer turned to fall, it was time for Magic and the rest of the Spartans to start thinking about the upcoming season. Everyone on campus was looking forward to it. Magic, Jay, and Greg were returning to the starting lineup. They were joined by Ron Charles, Mike Brkovich, and Terry Donnelly. Once again, the Spartans were expected to play a fast, running style of basketball designed to wear down their opponents. And Magic was expected to lead them.

Before Magic's sophomore season began, Coach Heathcote honored Magic by naming him one of the co-captains of the team. The Spartan coach realized that his sophomore superstar might well decide to turn professional after his second year, and Heathcote simply wanted to acknowledge Magic's contribution to the team as a player and a leader.

The Spartans got off to a fast start during the 1978–79 season. And they didn't look back. The Spartans finished the season with a 21–6 record and were again selected to play in the NCAA tournament. Michigan State rolled over their opponents in the opening rounds. They scored big victories over Lamar, Louisiana State University, and Notre Dame.

All of a sudden the Spartans were one of the "Final Four" teams that would be playing for the championship in Salt Lake City. Michigan State's opponent in the semifinal game was the University of Pennsylvania. The game was almost over before it began. By halftime, the Spartans were ahead 50–17. The second half wasn't any different, and the Spartans rolled to an easy victory.

The stage was set for Michigan State to play in the final for the national college basketball championship. Their opponent was the unbeaten team from Indiana State University. Indiana State had a record of 33–0 going into the championship game and were led by a kid named Larry Bird.

Basketball fans across the country were anxious to see these two superstars play against each other. The game attracted the largest crowd ever to attend a college game. Millions more Americans tuned in to watch the matchup between the two college superstars. Many college basketball fans, to this day, think that the game between Michigan State and Indiana State helped make college basketball the incredibly popular game it is today.

What fascinated everyone about the two players was their different styles. Larry Bird was an incredible shooter. Forwards usually do not have a very good outside shot, but Bird was an exception. He dazzled opponents with his ability to sink baskets from the outside. He could also pass the ball and, like Magic, possessed an incredible court sense.

Magic, on the other hand, was the ultimate playmaker on the court. He could control a game better than anyone. And his enthusiasm and attitude toward the game had attracted many fans.

Coach Heathcote knew that the Spartans would have to contain Bird if they had any hope of winning the game. In practice, before the championship, Heathcote told Magic to be Larry Bird. He knew that Magic could play against his own teammates as if he was the star from Indiana State. Heathcote wanted Magic to make it as hard as possible for his fellow Spartans to stop him.

Meanwhile, the pregame hype centered around the two superstars. Before the game, in a televised interview, Bird was reminded that he and Magic had played on the same team the summer before.

"You know, it's funny," smiled Bird, "Magic is such a great passer but he wouldn't pass me the ball, and I need the ball."

When told of Bird's comments, Magic flashed his famous smile and remarked, "Well I hope he doesn't think I'm going to pass him the ball tonight."

The stage was set for a classic championship match between two great basketball teams and two great basketball players.

As the contest began, the Spartans kept to their game plan of sticking to Bird closely so that he couldn't get off any easy shots. Throughout the first half, it was a close game.

In the second half, the Spartans began to pull ahead of the tiring Indiana State team. The final score was 75–64 in favor of Michigan State. The Spartans had held Bird to only 19 points (he had averaged 30 points a game until then) and

2 assists. The Michigan State Spartans were the 1979 national college basketball champions.

Although the two players would always be rivals on the court, Magic remembers the respect he felt for his rival that night. "Near the end when we were celebrating, he had his head in a towel, crying. Losing really hurt him and that's the sign of a true competitor." It had been the first, but not the last, of many classic games between the two basketball superstars.

The end of Magic's sophomore season meant once again having to decide whether to turn professional. On the one hand, he loved campus life and being a Spartan but, on the other hand, the team had won the national championship and he wanted so much to be a professional basketball player. Magic, his family, and Dr. Tucker once again began to discuss whether Magic should join the NBA.

While he was trying to decide what to do, Magic made a telephone call. He called Julius Erving, the famous Dr. J. of the Philadelphia 76ers, to ask for his advice. The two had met while Magic was at Michigan State. Dr. J. invited Magic to come to Philadelphia and watch the 76ers do battle in the NBA playoffs. The trip to Philadelphia made quite an impression on Magic.

"I kept tossing and turning. I thought about the whole college scene. The parties and the football games. Our games. How crazy the fans are. Then going to the pros. The glamour of the pros. I said, 'Wow, the NBA.' I wanted to play in the pros, bad."

Still, Magic couldn't make up his mind. At home, his parents were split on what decision their son should make. His mother, Christine, thought Junior should stay in school and get his degree, while his father thought the time was right for his son to turn pro. Dr. Tucker agreed with Earvin senior. When the Los Angeles Lakers got the first pick in the draft, they announced that Magic would be their choice if he was ready to leave school.

The thought of playing in Los Angeles excited Magic. Magic, his father, Dr. Tucker, and a lawyer hired by the family flew to Los Angeles to talk to the Lakers about Magic joining the team.

The talks, at first, didn't go very well. Magic, his family, and advisers thought he was worth a certain amount of money. The Lakers owner, Jack Kent Cooke, thought he was worth another amount. The two sides went back and forth for a couple of days until they finally reached an agreement. Magic would be paid $500,000 to become a Laker.

Magic returned to East Lansing to announce his decision to leave school and join the NBA. And to finish his final semester. His teammate Greg Kesler, a senior, had also become a professional player. He joined the Detroit Pistons. The two Spartan teammates bought cars for themselves and became familiar, if fleeting, sights on the East Lansing campus for a few weeks.

The draft was held in June of 1979 and it was then that Magic officially became a professional basketball player. The kid that had bounced a basketball on the streets of Lansing, taken his high school team to the state championship and his college team to the national championship, was going to be playing professional basketball for the Los Angeles Lakers. It was a long way from watching the Pistons on television and trying to get a big round orange basketball into a hoop that seemed so very high to a kid with nothing but dreams.

5
The Laker Years Begin

Imagine that you are a nineteen-year-old teen-ager and you are moving away from home for the first time. Oh sure, you had gone to Europe the summer before and taken other trips away from your family, but this was different. You were moving to a big city, Los Angeles, and you were signing a contract to play professional bas-ketball with the Lakers. What do you do? You take your father. Who knows, there might be a driveway somewhere there that could be used for a quick game of one-on-one.

So Earvin senior went out to Los Angeles with his son in late June of 1979 when Magic signed his first contract with the Lakers. Magic was, after all, still a teenager.

There was a lot of publicity surrounding the signing of Magic's contract. Reporters jammed into the press room of the Great Western Forum where the contract-signing ceremony was held. The reporters wanted to know how Magic thought he would adjust to being in the NBA. The youngster stated that he didn't think there was a big difference between playing in the pros and playing in college. "I enjoy playing basketball," he told the sportswriters. "Every game I play is fun. That's not going to change. My game plan is to have fun with a capital F-U-N. That's all, just have fun."

After the contract-signing ceremony was completed and the sportswriters had left, Magic went into the Forum's court. It was silent. The loud din of the reporters' questions rang in his ear as he took a seat up in the spectators' section. Slowly, the noises inside his head changed from the loud voices of the reporters to the roar of a packed house watching him play for the Lakers.

Magic sat there and imagined himself running up and down the floor of the Forum in his purple and yellow Laker uniform as the crowd cheered him and the Lakers to victory. The cheers, the shouts, the roar of the Los Angeles crowd filled his head. He couldn't wait to bounce the big orange ball on the hardwood court. Basketball season couldn't come soon enough for the NBA's newest sensation.

But first, Magic had to deal with Los Angeles and he was nervous about living in such a big city. "It was scary. Even with all the publicity, I thought I could handle the basketball part. But the city, I wasn't so sure about," said Magic upon looking back at his first days in California.

One of the first things Magic had to do was find a place to live. While a student at Michigan State, Magic had paid $250 a month for an off-campus apartment. He soon found out that the same size apartment in Los Angeles could cost as much as $1,000 a month. Magic eventually found a small apartment not far from the Los Angeles airport.

The publicity surrounding Magic's joining the Lakers started almost the day he arrived in Los Angeles. Dr. Tucker noticed, while spending a couple of weeks with Magic, that he was already recognized by people on the street and was being asked for his autograph.

When Magic reported to preseason camp, some of the veteran Lakers questioned his enthusiasm for the game. They had heard him say that each game for him was going to be fun. Veteran player Kareem Abdul-Jabbar smiled to himself when he thought about Magic's "fun" statement. Jabbar had been a college player at UCLA during the 1960s when they were unbeatable. And, after ten seasons as a professional basketball player, he knew the difference between college basketball and playing in the NBA. There were about three times as many games a season, a lot of traveling, and the games were longer with a faster pace. Jabbar loved playing basketball but he also knew how tiring it could be and that, sometimes, like anything else, it was a job.

So when the Lakers met for preseason practice, Jabbar, like the rest of the Lakers, waited for Magic's enthusiasm and energy to tire during the grueling two-a-day practice schedule. To their surprise, Magic did not tire or become less enthusiastic. He worked hard in practice, learning the style of the Lakers and trying to fit in as a member of the team.

The Lakers soon had a new nickname for the kid from Lansing, Michigan. None of the Lakers ever called him Magic. At first they called him by his given name, Earvin. But after watching him practice and play in games, the Laker veterans named the rookie "Buck." It was short for "young Buck." The rookie had reminded his teammates of a young buck because he was so full of energy and he practiced as if each drill and scrimmage game meant a world championship.

Magic's first game as a Laker was an exhibition game a month after he signed his contract. The NBA has a rookie league that plays a few games during the summer, and it was during one of these exhibition games that Laker fans first saw Magic in action.

The game was held in the gym at California State University. For these rookie games, about 1,000 people usually showed up to get a look at the new players. In this game, with Magic and the other Laker rookies meeting the first-year players from the Detroit Pistons, more than 3,000 fans crowded into the small college gymnasium. And hundreds of others were left outside not able to get in to see the game. Laker assistant coach Jack McCloskey was the coach for the game, and he didn't start Magic. But not long after the game started, McCloskey signaled for Magic to get off the bench and enter the game. The crowd was excited and eager to see what this kid from Michigan State would do with a basketball, and Magic didn't disappoint. Playing 28 minutes, Magic scored 24 points and made 9 assists.

His performance had Laker fans eagerly awaiting the regular season.

There was more of preseason camp to get through before the regular season started, and Coach Jack McKinney was busy figuring out how to blend his rookie into the veteran Laker lineup.

McKinney knew Magic's strength as a rebounder and ball controller. He immediately set up an offense that allowed for Magic to bring the ball up court fast after grabbing a defensive rebound. Usually, when a guard grabs a defensive rebound, he passes it off to the other guard who brings the ball up court to set up an offensive play. At the same time, the other team begins to set up its defense to prevent the offensive team from scoring. Because of Magic's speed and ability to accurately throw a full-court pass,

McKinney had him either bring the ball up court by himself — fast — or loft a full-court pass to an open teammate under the Laker basket.

Coach McKinney was taking advantage of Magic's speed and the speed possessed by the other Laker starters.

Forwards Jamal Wilkes and Jim Chones were also able to execute a fast break and could often outrun the men defending them and get open under the basket. As the center, Jabbar moved quickly and was able to position himself tight under the opposite backboard. The Laker's other guard, Norm Nixon, was an effective outside shooter. When bringing the ball up court, if Magic couldn't find an open man under the basket, he could pass it off to Nixon. Nixon was so smooth that, when he took a pass from Magic, he could receive the ball, set himself, and let go with a Laker basket — all in one fluid motion. That talent got him the name "Silk" from his teammates.

McKinney had found an effective way to utilize all the talents of his starting players. The fast-break offense that McKinney established with the Lakers often scored before their opponents knew what hit them. This fast and furious style of basketball became known as "Showtime." Every time Magic pulled down a defensive rebound and the Lakers began their fast break to the basket, the Forum crowd yelled, "It's Showtime!"

The Lakers opened the 1979–80 season in San

Diego against the Clippers. (The Clippers later moved to Los Angeles and became crosstown rivals of the Lakers.) Magic did not want to repeat his history of being nervous in his first game as he had been at Everett High and Michigan State.

He didn't. He handled the ball like a veteran and made several impressive passes to his open teammates under the boards.

But it wasn't Magic's playing that his fellow Laker teammates remember from his first game with the team. It was something that he did at the end of the game.

Just before the final buzzer, Jabbar let loose with his trademark over-the-shoulder sky hook that went through the basket and won the game for the Lakers. Magic could not contain his excitement. He leaped into Jabbar's arms and started to hug the man who had made the winning basket. Everyone was surprised. But Magic was just so excited that his Lakers had won the game. Soon his teammates joined in the celebration looking like a bunch of high school kids who had won a state championship instead of cool professional basketball players.

The person most surprised was Jabbar himself. When Magic finally settled down, Jabbar smiled at the rookie and said quietly, "Hey, we've still got 81 more of these."

But Magic's enthusiasm was hard to squelch. In time, he did save his celebrations for exceptional plays and last-minute victories. And soon,

Jabbar, who was seen as an unemotional player, began smiling and giving his teammates high fives after an outstanding play.

Early in the season, Coach McKinney had an accident while riding his bicycle. He hurt his head and was replaced by assistant coach Paul Westhead. The new head coach kept the fast-paced style of Showtime basketball and, by the end of Magic's rookie season, the Lakers were in the NBA playoffs.

As the Lakers entered the playoffs, Jabbar talked about what Magic meant to the Laker team. "Earvin had a very idealistic view of things when he came in. But my only concern was how he worked with the team. As soon as I saw the talent he had, I knew there was no way there'd be any problem. He always plays unselfishly, the way I always felt the game should be played. He has the perfect blend of attitude and talent."

Magic's attitude and talent, along with the talent of his teammates, helped the Lakers reach the NBA finals against the Philadelphia 76ers. It was a hard fought series and, after five games of the best-of-seven series, the Lakers were leading three games to two.

But during the fifth game, Jabbar sprained his ankle. He was able to finish the game and help the Lakers win to lead the series, but it soon became obvious that he would not be able to play in Game 6 in Philadelphia.

It looked like the Lakers had received a crushing blow to their chances to win Game 6 and the championship. The Lakers, the local sports-writers, and the fans just hoped that Jabbar's ankle would heal and that he would be able to play in Game 7. Everyone was pretty sure that the Lakers would not be able to win Game 6 without Jabbar. Well, not everyone. One person had total confidence that the Lakers could win Game 6 and become NBA champs.

On the plane to Philadelphia, Magic sat in the seat that was usually reserved for Jabbar. He wanted his teammates to know that he was willing and able to fill the shoes of the veteran. In fact, when Coach Paul Westhead asked the rookie to play center, Magic flashed the coach his famous smile and said, "No problem, Paul. I played some center in high school. It's beautiful to be in a situation like this. It's going to be enjoyable." Once again, Magic was looking forward to a challenge for his basketball talents.

The fans at the Spectrum in Philadelphia were surprised when Magic walked to center court and took Jabbar's position for the opening tip-off. They couldn't believe that Magic was playing center. A sigh of relief could almost be heard from the 76er fans in the Spectrum. They assumed that there was no way the Lakers could win with a rookie guard playing center.

Their sigh of relief immediately turned to a gasp. Magic controlled the tip-off, took a pass from a teammate, and drove the lane to make an easy lay-up for the game's first basket. For the next four periods, Magic put on a show that basketball fans still talk about to this day.

Magic continued to control the game. He played center, but his own style of center. Since he was known around the league as a superb passer, and not as an effective scorer, Magic played the center position as if he were playing guard. Instead of positioning himself under the backboard, he stayed outside. The 76ers, convinced that the rookie couldn't shoot effectively from the outside, left him open. The Lakers passed Magic the ball and he buried shot after shot from the outside. And in the process, he buried the 76ers.

Although the game was close for the first two periods, and was tied 60–60 at halftime, the Lakers began the third period by scoring 14 straight points.

But the 76ers kept the game close in the final period and closed the score to 103–101. The Lakers then outscored Philadelphia 20–6 in the final minutes of the contest and won the game 123–107. The Los Angeles Lakers had won their first NBA title since the 1971–72 season, four games to two.

For Magic it was the game of a lifetime. His statistics were incredible. He had scored 42 points, to the amazement of the fans and his teammates who didn't consider him a point maker. And his other statistics showed how important a part he had played in the victory. Magic ended up with 15 rebounds, 7 assists, 3 steals, while sinking all of his 14 free throws.

In celebrating the victory, while being interviewed on television, Magic had a message for his injured teammate back in Los Angeles. "Big fella, I did it for you. I know your ankle hurts, but I want you to get up and dance."

The Lakers had won the championship but, more importantly, Magic had established himself as a leader. At the age of twenty he had played like a seasoned professional, stepping in to Jabbar's shoes and leading the team to the NBA title.

And for Magic, it was his third championship in four years. In 1977, Magic led the Everett High Vikings to the state championship. In 1979, he led the Michigan State Spartans to the national college championship. And in 1980, Magic had spearheaded the Lakers to the NBA crown.

The night of the Laker victory over Philadelphia, former NBA star, Rick Barry, who had witnessed Magic's amazing performance, shook his head in wonder. "He thinks every season ends this way," said Barry. "You go to training camp, play a few games, go to the playoffs, then win a championship. It's unbelievable. Absolutely unbelievable."

It had been a dream season for the rookie guard from Michigan. Magic had played in 77 regular season games, averaging 18.0 points, 7.7 rebounds, and over 7 assists per game. In one year, he had established himself as a superstar in the NBA. The future looked bright for Magic.

There seemed no reason why he wouldn't be a large part of a Laker dynasty. Magic and the rest of the Lakers looked forward to the 1980–81 season and a repeat as NBA champs. Little did Magic, or the rest of the Lakers, know that the 1980–81 season would be one of the most disappointing for Magic and his Los Angeles teammates.

6
Ups and Downs with the Lakers

Imagine you are entering your second year in the NBA. Your rookie year had been a dream season and had ended with your team winning the NBA championship. Everyone was looking forward to what you could do to top that rookie season. The pressure was on you and your team-mates to win another championship.

For the first time in his career, Magic was not playing for an underdog. His fans weren't hoping for another championship — they *expected* it.

When preseason camp opened for the 1980–81 season, the Lakers set the goal of becoming the first team since the 1968–69 Boston Celtics to repeat as NBA champions. The mood in camp was upbeat. All the players were looking forward to another season of Laker "Showtime" basketball.

Then Coach Westhead made a surprise announcement. He was changing the fast-paced offense of the Lakers. Instead of having the same player who pulled down a defensive rebound quickly bring the ball up court, he was slowing down the offense by having the rebounder pass the ball to a teammate. That player would then bring the ball up court slowly as his teammates went to set positions near or under the basket. Westhead outlined several different offensive plays.

This news was met with little enthusiasm by the team, but each player understood that, as Coach, Westhead was the man in charge.

As the season began, Westhead's new offensive plan was working. In the first few weeks of the season, they had run up a 15-5 record. And Magic was having an even better season than his remarkable rookie year. He was averaging 21.4 points a game and was leading the league in steals and assists. Magic was also leading all guards in rebounds with 8.2 per game.

Then, on November 11, 1980, Tom Burleson, of the Atlanta Hawks, fell across the back of Magic's knee. At first no one even knew that Magic had been injured. He even played in a couple of more games until, one night, he could hear a clicking sound in his leg every time he took a step. Then his knee began to feel stiff.

When Dr. Robert Kerlan, the Laker's physician, examined the leg he discovered that Magic had torn cartilage in his knee. It would require surgery. And although the surgery was considered minor, it kept Magic out of action for the next 45 Laker games.

Without their enthusiastic leader and playmaker, the Lakers lost five of their next eight games. But as much as the Lakers missed Magic, the young superstar missed being part of the team even more.

"It made me see that, just as fast as you can rise to the top, you can come tumbling down," Magic said when he returned to the Laker lineup in February of 1981. "First they take your ball away. That's bad. And then, not being around the guys, that really hurts. I mean, you're all alone now, you see. . . . That's my life, being around the fellas, talking jive, singing on the bus, that's the whole thing. All of a sudden that was all taken away. I don't think missing the ball was that important. Missing the fellas was badder than missing the ball."

Magic's leg was put in a cast for the first two weeks following the surgery. As soon as he was able to walk around without crutches, Magic went to the Forum to sit on the bench and watch his teammates play.

What he saw that night disturbed him. The Lakers had lost their previous five games, and Westhead had made some changes in the lineup, benching starters Michael Cooper and Jim Chones. Magic could understand how a coach might want to make some changes, especially during a losing streak. But he also noticed that these players were unhappy and that their unhappiness was because Coach Westhead had not explained to them his reasons for benching them. The players sat and fumed. Magic could see things were changing while he was out with his knee injury.

Magic also visited his family and friends while his knee was recovering. As much as Magic was beginning to like life in Los Angeles, he enjoyed going home to Lansing. "I miss the community, the hominess of it," Magic said about the difference between Lansing and Los Angeles. "There everybody knows each other. You call people up, and in five minutes you got a softball game together. I like that. I miss it."

Even so, Magic was adjusting to life in Los Angeles. He was a star and everywhere he went people wanted to talk to him or get an autograph. Even when Magic was driving in his Mercedes Benz, people would stare at him and wave on the Los Angeles freeways. It got so that people were constantly honking their horns at him. Magic finally had the windows of his car tinted so he could drive in peace.

Magic returned to the Laker lineup at the Great Western Forum in late February. The fans wore buttons that read THE MAGIC IS BACK and gave their hero a 45-second standing ovation. (One second for each game he had missed.)

The night Magic returned, the Lakers were

playing the New Jersey Nets. With 5:02 left in the first period, Coach Westhead sent Magic into the game, and the crowd in the Forum waited for the magic to begin. It took a while for the young superstar to get his form back, and he made some mistakes in those first few minutes. Then something happened that had the fans silent with fear. Magic collided violently with Maurice Lucas of the Nets while going for a loose ball. Everyone in the Forum held their breath until Magic lifted himself up easily — and smiled.

"I'm glad he knocked me down," Magic said after the game. "I need to be knocked around."

In typical Magic style, he showed that he hadn't come back to play basketball only halfway. He had come back fully to play the complete game with all the shoving, pushing, and colliding.

With Magic back, the Lakers continued their quest for a second straight NBA crown. They finished the season with a 54–28 record, good enough for a second place in the Pacific Division and a spot in the playoffs.

The Lakers met the Houston Rockets in the first round. Houston had barely made it in to the playoffs having won only 40 games while losing 42 during the regular season.

But the Rockets played hard against the Lakers and, after two games in the best-of-three series, each team had won a game. The deciding game, to see who would advance in the playoffs, was played at the Forum. Just as everyone had thought the Lakers would surely lose Game 6 of the finals the year before, everyone now thought the Lakers would beat the Rockets and advance to the next round of the playoffs. This year, the pressure was on the team in yellow and purple.

And the pressure became too much. The Lakers were upset by the lowly Rockets who won the game 89–86. The Laker season was over and they would not repeat as champions. What made it worse for Magic was the fact that he missed a jump shot near the end of the game that could have won it for the Lakers.

It was a disappointing loss for the Lakers and for Magic. But then something happened that made Magic, the Lakers, and their fans forget all about the upset loss to Houston in the playoffs.

In June of 1981, Magic signed a new contract with the team. The contract was for 25 years and $25 million. At the time, there had never been a contract like this offered to a professional athlete.

Everyone knew that Magic wouldn't play basketball for twenty-five years. What the young basketball star was doing was insuring his future with the Lakers, not only as a player, but as a businessman as well.

Magic had not let go of his dream of being a successful businessman. The kid who had dreamed of owning his own company while he cleaned office buildings had turned into a man who wanted to play an important part in the business dealings of the Los Angeles Lakers when his playing days were over.

Magic's dream was coming true. As far as Laker owner Jerry Buss was concerned, Magic would be with the Lakers for a long time. He knew that the man wearing number 32 on his Lakers' uniform could also be an asset wearing a business suit.

When he was asked about what Magic could do for the Lakers once he stopped playing, Buss said, "He may be my coach. Or general manager. Or maybe he'll run the team and I'll just sit back and watch."

When the Lakers reported to preseason camp before the 1981–82 season, Westhead announced that he would continue the same slow-paced offense he had used the season before. As Magic's third season began, he became more and more frustrated by Westhead's style of coaching. Eleven games into the season, Magic announced to a newspaper reporter that he wanted to be traded. It was a stunning announcement. Especially since his $25 million, 25-year contract was only a few months old.

The Lakers did not trade their superstar. Instead, they fired their coach. Immediately, some of the fans and sportswriters thought Magic, because of his new powerful contract, had been able to get Westhead fired. It simply wasn't true.

Dr. Buss was as much a basketball fan as he was an owner, and he missed the fast "Showtime" style of Laker basketball that had characterized Magic's rookie season. He had been disappointed by the loss in the playoffs to Houston and felt a faster-paced game could have beaten the Rockets. He told reporters that he had been planning on firing Westhead since the end of the previous season.

The fans didn't buy it. They resented that Magic, a 22-year-old kid, was making millions of dollars and was powerful enough to get his coach fired. They didn't seem to care whether it was true or not. Owner Jerry Buss assured the Lakers, and Magic, that the decision to fire Westhead was his and his alone.

Pat Riley, who had been an assistant coach under Westhead, was named the new head coach. He brought back the fast style of "Showtime" basketball in his first practice.

The night the Lakers played their first game at the Forum under Coach Riley, the team was not ready for the reception that Magic received when he was introduced in the starting lineup. The crowd began to boo. And they continued as Magic stood at center court, not letting up.

It was a devastating moment for Magic. He couldn't believe his ears and he couldn't stop the tears from welling up in his eyes. As the rest of his teammates were introduced, Magic became determined to win back the Laker fans.

It didn't take long. Against the visiting San

Antonio Spurs, the Lakers soon began working their fast breaks, and the crowd got excited. As the Lakers pulled ahead of the Spurs, and it became obvious that "Showtime" was back, the boos turned to cheers.

"That was the toughest time I ever went through," Magic said later about that first game after Coach Westhead was fired.

Magic also came to realize that he shouldn't have used the media to announce that he wanted to be traded. "I know now I should have kept my feelings to myself," Magic said years later. "I didn't mean for Westhead to be fired. I guess I was naive to think I would be traded before the coach was fired but, at the time, I honestly was ready to play somewhere else."

With Pat Riley as their new coach, the Lakers won 11 of their next 13 games and eventually defeated the Philadelphia 76ers in six games to win their second NBA title in three years. Magic was named the Most Valuable Player in the championship series. The cheers for Magic and the Lakers were back for good.

7
Magic Finds a House and Meets Bird in the Finals

Imagine you are in your fourth year as a professional basketball player. You are known as one of the leading players in the NBA. Everywhere you go in Los Angeles, people wave and smile at you. But something is missing. You are still living in an apartment and you want to buy a house. One you can call your very own.

The fact is, Magic had been looking for a house since moving to Los Angeles. He would often go with Dr. Tucker to look at homes while Dr. Tucker was visiting. Finally, Magic saw his dream house. It was the first house of several he was scheduled to see one particular day.

"I had been looking for a house for a long time. On the day I picked this, I had a list of several to look at. But this was the first on the list. When

I saw it, I knew this was the place for me," Magic said, recalling the day.

It was a large, Tudor-style house that looked as if it belonged nestled in the English country-side instead of the Los Angeles suburb of Bel Air. It had five bedrooms, five bathrooms, and a three-car garage. Plus, there was a swimming pool and tennis courts in the large backyard.

Before he moved in, Magic wanted to make some changes inside the house. He had an in-door basketball court put in so he could shoot hoops anytime he wanted. The backboard was on runners that could be raised when the court was used for racquetball or volleyball games.

Magic also turned one of the rooms into a party room, with forty colored lights, that could hold 150 dancers. "I had the party area specially designed so I could continue as EJ the DJ," Magic would say when showing the room to friends.

Since Magic was still a bachelor, he didn't need five bedrooms but he did want there to be plenty of room so his friends and family could visit. Magic even named three of the bedrooms for three of his favorite people.

There was the Christine room, named after his mother. There was the Isiah room, named after his good friend Isiah Thomas of the Detroit Pistons. And there was the Tuck room, named after Dr. Charles Tucker.

Magic also hired a housekeeper after he moved in. Besides helping keep the big house tidy, Leola Manning, the housekeeper, cooked Magic's meals. It wasn't as big a job as she expected. "He eats very little for a man as big as he is," the housekeeper said of Magic's eating habits.

Magic loved his new house. He used the jacuzzi and enjoyed the stereo system with speakers in every room. But soon, Magic noticed that one more thing was needed to make his new house a real home.

In the backyard there was a tennis court. On one end of the tennis court, Magic wanted a backboard so he could shoot hoops just like he had done with his father in the family driveway in Lansing. One end of the tennis court was at the very edge of the backyard. Just past that edge was a valley that was several hundred feet deep.

When the contractor showed up to install the backboard, he suggested to Magic that he place the backboard on the opposite side of the tennis court, away from the valley. That way, said the contractor, Magic wouldn't lose any balls into the valley if he missed the backboard.

"Put it on the valley side," Magic said. "Magic Johnson doesn't miss."

Magic was busy shooting baskets in his home and in the LA Forum. As the 1982–83 season began, the Lakers were hoping to win their third title in four years.

Their hopes were buoyed by the fact that they had a new rookie sensation, James Worthy. He had been an outstanding player for the University of North Carolina Tarheels. And like Magic, he had led his team to the NCAA championship. Worthy also liked the Laker style of basketball and soon became a valuable member of the team.

The season started at home against the Golden State Warriors. The rings for their championship of the previous year were handed out. Then the Lakers went out and lost their first game. But they soon got back on a winning track. And so did Magic.

During his fourth season with the Lakers, Magic had 829 assists, leading the league and breaking former-Laker Jerry West's record for assists in one season. The 1982–83 season was also the first of eight consecutive seasons that Magic would be named to the All-NBA First Team.

The Lakers finished the season with a 58–24 record, good enough to win the Pacific Division. But all was not good news for the Lakers. Just before they were to begin the playoffs against the Portland Trailblazers, rookie James Worthy broke his leg and was lost for the championship quest.

The Lakers, without Worthy, defeated the Trailblazers in five games. Their next opponent was the San Antonio Spurs and, in a hard fought series, the Lakers turned them back in six games. They were off to the NBA finals once again against the Philadelphia 76ers.

Moses Malone had joined the 76ers as an

imposing center. Malone and the rest of the Philadelphia team proved too much for the Lakers. They swept the Los Angeles squad in four straight games.

During the off-season, the Lakers traded guard Norm Nixon. Though Magic and Norm worked well together, they were both basically point guards. This sometimes made for an awkward situation that was fixed by trading Norm and making Magic the one and only Laker point guard.

The Lakers got Byron Scott for Nixon. Scott was better known as a shooting guard. With Magic in the role of play caller and ball handler, he now played with a guard that was more talented at shooting than controlling the ball.

The addition of Scott in the backcourt worked well for the Lakers. And for Magic. During the 1983–84 season, Magic led the league and made a career-high 875 assists. And in the 1984 All-Star Game, Magic had 22 assists to break the record for the NBA's mid-season showcase.

But he wasn't the only Laker to shine. Kareem Abdul-Jabbar broke Wilt Chamberlain's all-time scoring record in April of 1984.

And for the third time in five years, the Lakers were in the NBA finals. And this time they were playing their archrivals, the Boston Celtics, who were led by Larry Bird. Once again, as they had in 1979 for the NCAA title, Magic and Larry were meeting for a basketball championship.

The two had played in ten regular-season games against each other during their first five years as pros. Since Los Angeles is in the Western Conference and Boston is in the Eastern Conference, they only played against each other twice each season.

Every time the Lakers and Celtics played, the players and the fans treated each game as if it were for the championship. This was partly due to Magic and Larry. But it was also due to the rivalry between the teams that went back many years.

Between 1959 and 1969, the Celtics and the Lakers played each other seven times for the NBA title. The Celtics won all seven. Fans of both teams were aware of this history between the clubs, and that made each contest more exciting.

In the ten regular-season games during the first five seasons Magic was with the Lakers, the teams each won five games. And each time the teams met, newspapers were filled with articles comparing Magic and Larry.

The two superstars did not know each other off the court during their early years in the NBA. Before the Celtics and Lakers met in the finals, Larry said, "I don't go out to dinner with him. I just know him on the basketball floor, and that's it." Magic said pretty much the same thing about Larry, "I still don't know him very well."

The two stars did respect each others' ability on the court. And many people, including David

Stern, commissioner of the NBA, considered Magic and Larry the two best players in the league. Stern said, "Put fifty basketball minds in a room and ask them to pick a player to start their team. Twenty-five of them will choose Bird and the other twenty-five will choose Magic."

The stage was set for a classic championship series between two teams that were bitter rivals, and two superstar players.

The series opened in Boston, and the Lakers played their famous fast-break style of basketball to beat the Celtics on their home court. And in Game 2, also played in the Boston Garden, it looked like the Lakers had another victory.

Los Angeles was leading by two points with just a few seconds left in the game. It looked like the Lakers would return to Los Angeles for the next game with a 2–0 lead in the series. But then Magic made not one mistake, but two.

Teammate James Worthy was ready to inbound the ball. It was Magic's job to come in toward the ball to receive the pass. He didn't, and when the pass came in, Gerald Henderson of the Celtics stole it and scored an easy basket to tie the game.

There were still a few seconds left and it was up to Magic to once again take the inbound pass. This time he got the ball, but he just froze as time ran out. "I didn't know what to do. I just blanked out," remembers Magic when talking about this low point in his career.

The Celtics won that game in overtime and

the series moved to the Forum in Los Angeles. The Lakers trounced the Celtics in the third game 137–104, and Magic set an NBA record for most assists in a championship-series game with 21.

Game 4 was also played in Los Angeles, and the Lakers found themselves once again in a position to take a two-game lead with only seconds left on the clock. And once again, to everyone's amazement, it was Magic who made the mistake that cost the Lakers the game. The score was tied — 116–116 — and the Lakers had the ball. Magic dribbled the ball up court as the Lakers set up an offensive play that would allow Magic to either pass to Worthy or make his own offensive move. But Magic became very cautious with the ball and allowed too much time to go by on the clock. He finally passed to Worthy, but it was knocked out-of-bounds by Celtic center Robert Parrish.

The game went into overtime and, with 35 seconds left and the score tied, Magic was fouled. He stepped to the line and missed both shots. It was unbelievable considering Magic was making 81 percent of his free throws throughout the playoffs. Larry Bird grabbed the rebound, took the ball down court, and scored. The Celtics had tied the series at two games apiece.

The Celtics won game five in Los Angeles and took a 3–2 lead in the best-of-seven series back to their home court, the famed Boston Garden.

But the Lakers did not lay down and die in Game 6. They beat the Celtics to force a seventh and deciding game.

The Celtics opened a commanding 14-point lead early in the game, to the delight of their screaming fans. But the Lakers hung in there and closed to within three points of Boston late in the game. As Magic dribbled the ball down court, he saw Worthy open near the basket. But before he could pass the ball, Boston's Cedric Maxwell stole it. As the final seconds ticked, Maxwell just held the ball. The Celtics had won the title.

It was, without a doubt, the lowest point of Magic's professional basketball career. He felt it was his fault that the Lakers had lost Games 2 and 4. Games that would have given the Lakers a two-game cushion over their rivals from Boston.

All summer long, Magic blamed himself for the Lakers not winning the championship. The sportswriters in Los Angeles helped Magic keep the disappointing series in mind. Articles with headlines like EARVIN, WHAT HAPPENED TO MAGIC? hinted that maybe Magic wasn't as magical a player as everyone thought.

His mother, Christine, had never liked the nickname Magic. When it was first given to her son, she said the name would make people think that her son could do everything on the basketball court. Now, she noticed, when her son came to visit Lansing, he didn't smile as much. She feared he was taking too much of the blame for the playoff loss. But, at the same time, she noted a new look of determination on Magic's face.

There were also reports that Magic's head was getting too big for him — especially with his $25-million contract and his alleged role in the firing of Coach Westhead. Teammate Jabbar quickly came to Magic's defense. He pointed out that Magic was the first player on the team to pass to another player instead of making the basket himself.

By the time the Lakers reported to preseason camp for the 1984–85 season, Magic had put the loss to the Celtics behind him. Magic and the rest of the Lakers were determined to regain the NBA title.

The Lakers began the season strong and soon showed the rest of the NBA that they were one of the league's best teams. The newspaper reports from the previous summer were soon forgotten. Magic was as popular as ever. He received 957,447 votes from the fans for the 1985 All-Star Game. And Magic led the West All-Stars to their first win in five years over the East All-Stars.

Magic loved playing in All-Star games with the other leading players of the league. And the other All-Stars loved playing with Magic. His All-Star teammate Ralph Sampson of the Houston Rockets said after the 1985 game, "What I enjoyed most was playing with Magic. He has great court awareness."

The second half of the season was remarkable for the Lakers. They won thirty-one of their final thirty-five games, including seventeen in a row at home in the Forum. They finished on top of the Pacific Division, twenty games ahead of the second-place team. Magic broke his own career record by making 968 assists during the season. But what he wanted most of all was another chance to play Boston in the NBA finals.

The Celtics had won their division, so there was potential for a rematch. The Lakers made it possible by beating the Phoenix Suns, Portland Trailblazers, and Denver Nuggets to reach the finals. Boston did their part by defeating the Cleveland Cavaliers, Detroit Pistons, and Philadelphia 76ers. The stage was set for Round Two of the Lakers versus the Celtics, and Magic Johnson versus Larry Bird.

Game 1 was in Boston, and the Celtics won big, 148–114. It didn't look like the Lakers would avenge their 1984 championship loss to Boston. But the Lakers won Game 2 in Boston Garden to even the series. The series moved to Los Angeles for the next three games, and the Lakers took two of them to lead the series, 3–2, after five games.

Game 6 was played in Boston Garden. It was hard for any team other than the Celtics to win in the Garden. The arena is old, and the visitor's locker room is quite small. The fans in Boston are extremely vocal and it is often hard for teams to hear their coaches instructions during time-outs — even when the team huddles close.

The Garden had always been a tough place for the Lakers to win. And it wasn't just the roar of the crowd. On many nights before a game with the Celtics, while the Lakers were fast asleep in their hotel rooms, the fire alarm would go off. The team, like the rest of the hotel guests, would be forced to get out of bed from a sound sleep, get dressed, and go outside, before the officials could be sure there was no fire.

There had been so many false alarms before Games 1 and 2 of the 1984 championship series, the Lakers had been forced to change hotels.

So it was with some concern that the Lakers entered Boston Garden for Game 6 of the 1985 championship series, even though they were leading the series by one game.

The Celtics had never lost a championship game in Boston Garden. But in Game 6, the Lakers got off to an early lead. And the Celtics just weren't hitting their outside shots. While they didn't totally destroy the Celtics, the Lakers did hold on to a comfortable lead throughout the game and eventually won, 111–100.

The Lakers were NBA champs for the third time in six years. But for Magic, and the rest of the Lakers, the victory was even sweeter because it proved that the Lakers could beat the Celtics on the Celtics home court.

"The sweetest sound I ever heard was the quiet

in the Garden when we took over the sixth game of the 1985 finals. In the last minutes, it went from thousands of people yelling for us to lose, to just quiet," Magic said once, when asked what it was like to play in Boston Garden.

The summer of 1985 was more pleasant for Magic than the previous one. Once again, he and the Lakers were heroes to their fans.

The Lakers reported to preseason camp before the 1985–86 season with basically the same team that had won the championship in June. Byron Scott and Magic were still the guards, Kareem was at center, and James Worthy was at forward. A. C. Green began to shine and he soon became the fifth Laker starter.

And the Lakers were facing their third opportunity in seven years to repeat as NBA champions. No NBA team had been able to accomplish that feat since the Celtics had won back-to-back championships in 1968 and 1969.

As the season began, it looked like the Lakers might finally achieve their goal of two consecutive NBA titles. They won 11 of their first 12 games, and 24 of their first 27. The entire team was on fire, especially Jabbar, the veteran center. In one game against the New York Knicks, he scored 40 points. A few nights later, he scored 46 against the Houston Rockets. Byron Scott was an effective shooter and Michael Cooper was used off the bench for his great defensive skills.

Magic was also having a fine year. In the first half of the season he lead the league in assists. When the ballots were counted for the 1986 All-Star Game, Magic became the first player in history to receive more than a million votes from the fans.

During the second half of the season, in a game on March 13, 1986, Magic made his 5,000th career assist. And when the regular season ended, Magic once again led the league in assists.

The Lakers ended the season in a familiar spot — on top of the Pacific Division of the Western Conference. The Celtics won their division as well and everyone looked forward to the third straight Los Angeles–Boston NBA final.

The Lakers rolled to the Western Conference championship series against the Houston Rockets. The Lakers, as in 1981, were favored to beat the Rockets and advance to the finals. During the 1985–86 regular season, the Lakers had beaten the Rockets in four of five games.

In the first game, the Lakers won 119–107, and Jabbar scored 31 points. It was the last Laker victory of the season, though. Houston stormed back and took four straight from the Lakers to crush their chances of repeating as NBA champs.

This time, Magic didn't let defeat get him down. Instead, he turned his attention to a very special basketball game that would raise a small fortune for one of his favorite causes — The United Negro College Fund.

8
Magic the Fund-Raiser

Imagine that you are truly a superstar in the NBA. You are recognized as one of the best players in the game, you have become rich beyond your wildest dreams, you live in the perfect house, and you count among your friends movie stars and powerful people in business and politics. What do you do to make your life even better?

For Magic, the answer to that question was simple. In the summer of 1986, not long after the disappointing loss to the Houston Rockets in the Western Conference finals, Magic decided to hold a fund-raiser for one of his favorite organizations — The United Negro College Fund (UNCF).

One night, Magic had attended a dinner to benefit the UNCF. After the dinner, he said to himself, "Hey, why am *I* not having some sort of dinner?"

Magic's dinner for the UNCF quickly became more than a meal. He added a basketball game as part of his benefit and called the evening, "A Midsummer Night's Magic." He personally invited some of his superstar friends from the NBA to play in this very special basketball game. Magic decided that the game would be played following the dinner, and he began to sell tickets to the event.

"A Midsummer Night's Magic" has raised more than $5 million in the six years that it has been held. And each year, Magic does more than just show up to play an exhibition basketball game. Much more. He oversees every detail of the game and the dinner, from the seating arrangements for dinner to hotel rooms for the NBA superstars who play in the games. His involvement is hands-on. And not only with the players.

One time when he was on vacation in Hawaii he met a fan on the beach. Magic told the woman about his charity basketball game. She made a contribution. When Magic got back to Los Angeles, he personally sent her a thank-you note. And when the woman's birthday arrived, so did a card from Magic.

He made sure that this woman knew her contribution was appreciated. Now, the woman sends in a contribution of more than $100,000 every year.

It is that kind of attention to detail that impresses Vincent M. Bryson, Southern California director of development for the UNCF. "People's motivations for doing good work are sometimes suspect. But Magic has the most unselfish attitude I've ever seen. He is not interested in promoting himself."

Magic's involvement with charities goes beyond the UNCF annual fund-raiser. He sponsors a program for kids in Lansing who have reading difficulties. Magic also hosts a celebrity golf tournament that raises about $200,000 for the American Heart Association. He has also remained active with the Boys Clubs of America, an organization he did volunteer work for as a kid in Lansing.

Magic donates his basketball shoes and his basketballs to charities trying to raise money. He has also taken part in charity celebrity one-on-one games. Why does he do it? "I can't understand players who don't get involved with charities and in their communities. Somebody helped them out once. I know somebody helped me out and I don't ever want to forget."

With all the time spent organizing and hosting his first "A Midsummer Night's Magic " in 1986, Magic had also been asked by Coach Riley to help out the Lakers in a new role.

With the end of the 1986 season came the realization that the Lakers top scorer, Kareem Abdul-Jabbar, would not be playing for too many more years. It was time for the Lakers to adjust their game to compensate for the eventual loss of their superstar center. Riley wrote to Magic that summer and asked him to work on his shooting.

That is just what Magic did. He became determined to help the Lakers in his new role as a scoring threat. But he worried about how Jabbar, who had always been given the role of lead scorer for the team, would react to Coach Riley's suggestion. Magic called Jabbar, and the veteran assured him that he understood what Riley was trying to do and that the most important thing was the team.

The "new" Lakers began the 1986–87 season, and the fans were surprised to see Magic scoring more points. Because he had been so skilled at making assists (passing the ball to the player who then could made an easy shot), Laker fans just weren't used to seeing Magic take so many shots. And make them. Even though it was Magic who had scored 42 points in that important playoff game in Philadelphia that won the Lakers the championship in 1980.

For Magic and the Lakers, the 1986–87 season was one of many triumphs. For Magic, he led the Lakers in scoring with a 23.9 average per game. Once again he led the league in assists. But the biggest honor was given to Magic while the Lakers were still in the playoffs.

On May 18, 1987, Magic was named the Most Valuable Player in the NBA. He was thrilled. With typical grace and good humor, Magic accepted the award. "I'd like to thank Larry Bird for having a slightly off year, and I want to strangle Michael Jordan for putting all the pressure on me," he said holding the MVP trophy. Larry Bird had won the MVP award in the previous three seasons and Michael Jordan had been a close second to Magic in the MVP balloting. Then Magic turned serious. He dedicated his MVP trophy to his father. No one, said Magic, had been more of an influence in his life. No one had worked as hard.

As nice as the MVP trophy was, Magic wanted something else to remember that remarkable season by. A fourth NBA title for the Lakers.

In June of 1987, the Lakers were once again in the NBA championship series. Their opponents were none other than their rivals from the East Coast, the Boston Celtics. And once again, everyone talked about the matchup between Magic Johnson and Larry Bird.

But something had happened between the two superstars since they had last met in the 1985 championship series. While working together on a commercial for Converse shoes, they had gotten to know each other. What had been a mutual respect on the basketball court had become a true friendship off the hardwood floor.

"We found we had a lot in common," said Magic after he got to know Larry. "We're both from the Midwest, we like to go home in the off-season and see our folks. We found we really enjoyed each other. It would have been a shame if we'd never gotten to know each other as people, not just as basketball players."

It was during this championship series that Magic felt he made the shot of his career. It happened during the fourth game in the dreaded Boston Garden. The Lakers were leading the series two games to one. It was late in the game and the Celtics were ahead by one point. Magic had the ball with ten seconds left and decided to attempt a shot — one he called the junior sky hook.

It was Jabbar's sky hook that had won Magic's first game as a Laker back in 1979. The shot that caused the rookie to jump into Jabbar's arms in excitement. Magic saw the opportunity, and released the ball over his shoulder toward the basket. The ball arched over the outstretched arms of the Celtic defenders and went through the net for a Laker victory.

Once again, Magic and the Lakers heard the sweet sound in Boston Garden. Thousands of screaming Celtic fans had been silenced by defeat to the Lakers.

The Celtics won the next game to close the best-of-seven series to three games to two. But the Lakers won Game 6 and their fourth NBA title in eight years in front of their hometown fans at the Forum. Magic was named Most Valuable Player in the series to add to his MVP award for the regular season.

* * *

It had been a storybook season for Magic and the Lakers. The only thing that could top it was repeating as NBA champions in the 1987–88 season. Three times previously, since Magic joined the team, the Lakers had failed to repeat as champs. Once again, as the team gathered for preseason camp in 1987, the only thing on their mind was winning a second consecutive title.

The Lakers, known for their fast style of play, were becoming even more of a threat with Magic proving himself to be as effective a scorer as he was a passer.

The Lakers continued to dominate other teams that season. Opponents just couldn't keep up with their speed and agility. And although Magic didn't win an MVP award or lead the league in assists, he did make one memorable shot against the Celtics in the Boston Garden.

The game on December 11, 1987, was a typical Los Angeles–Boston matchup — close and physical. Just before the final buzzer, Magic let loose with a 20-foot jump shot that banked against the backboard and went through the net as the game ended.

For the third time in his career, Magic listened to the deafening noise of the Boston Garden go silent. The NBA doesn't keep statistics on how often a team, or a player, can quiet the crowd in the Garden but, for Magic, the three times he made the Celtic fans silent remain some of the sweetest memories of his NBA career.

But perhaps *the* sweetest memory was to come in the 1987–88 playoffs. After failing to repeat as NBA champions in three previous attempts, the Lakers finally won back-to-back championships.

The fact that the Lakers beat the Detroit Pistons for the championship was especially meaningful for Magic. His family still lived in Lansing, which was less than two hours from Detroit. And it was the Pistons, after all, that Magic had watched as a child as his father began to teach him the game of basketball.

During the series, when the games were being played in Detroit, Magic and the rest of the Lakers went to Lansing for a home-cooked meal prepared by Magic's mother.

The Lakers won a hard fought series by defeating the Pistons 108–105 in the seventh and deciding game. They became the first team in twenty years to repeat as NBA champions.

On June 22, Magic Johnson and his Laker teammates celebrated before 38,000 screaming fans on the steps of the Los Angeles City Hall. It was the Lakers fifth NBA title in nine years. The Lakers had established themselves as the dominant team of the 1980's. But would they be able to win the title again in 1989 for the third consecutive year?

9
Another Dream Comes True

Imagine you are twenty-eight years old. In your profession, professional basketball, twenty-eight is not considered young. Your knees are bothered by tendinitis and, after every game, you apply ice packs to relieve the aches and pains. What should you do?

What Magic did was to increase his off-season conditioning. He added running, cycling, and lifting weights to increase the strength in his knees. He also turned to the one player on his team who had played the longest and remained in top physical condition: Kareem Abdul-Jabbar.

The veteran center showed Magic some stretching exercises. Magic found that, at first, he hurt more after stretching than before. But Jabbar assured him that was to be expected, and

Magic stuck with the exercises. He figured if they were good enough for Jabbar, who had played longer than anyone in the NBA, they were good enough for him.

Magic's conditioning paid off. In his tenth year as a Laker, Magic once again led the team to the NBA finals. And for the second time in his career, Magic was named the Most Valuable Player of the regular season in the NBA. And as he had done after winning the MVP award in 1987, Magic dedicated his trophy to his father. "He is the reason I am on this earth," Magic said.

It was a title that Magic won in another category that season that surprised him the most. Magic ended the season with the best free-throw percentage in the league: an incredible .911 percent! It was especially satisfying to him because Magic still remembered the two free throws he missed during the 1984 championship series with Boston that could have won a critical game.

The Lakers once again reached the NBA finals in a return series with the Detroit Pistons. The Lakers were hoping to end their incredible decade with a sixth NBA title and their third in three years.

In Game 2, Magic went down with a hamstring injury. He started Game 3, but soon realized that he couldn't play basketball while limping. Four minutes into the game, Magic had to come out. He was finished playing basketball for the season.

The other Laker guard, Byron Scott, had also suffered a hamstring injury in a practice and couldn't play. With both first-string guards out with injuries, the Lakers were no match for the Pistons, and Detroit won the championship series four games to one.

The 1980's were over but it had been an impressive ten years for the team from Los Angeles. They had won five NBA championships and had been in the finals eight of the ten years.

And it wasn't just the decade that ended when the 1988–89 season was over. After twenty years in the NBA, Kareem Abdul-Jabbar retired from basketball. He left the game as the player who scored the most points (38,387), played the most games (1,560), and blocked the most shots (3,189).

To Magic, he was all that and more. Jabbar had been a great friend and teacher. He had taught Magic the skyhook and proper conditioning techniques. And, most important, through his example he taught Magic how to lead.

And now it was time for Magic to officially take over the leadership role of the Lakers. To many, it appeared that Magic already had been the leader. In his role as playmaker for the Los Angeles Lakers, he set up the offense. And his outgoing personality was that of a born leader. But the Lakers, and especially Magic, always looked to Jabbar as the leader of their team. Now it would be Magic who would take on that role.

Magic felt the pressure during that first season without Jabbar. "There's more pressure on me now than there's ever been. I have to perform every night for us to win. Even at this point in my career, I'm trying to make myself better. I go out every night thinking I will do whatever it takes — that night — for us to win."

Magic did just that. The 1990's picked up where the 1980's had left off for the Lakers and for Magic. For the eleventh time in eleven seasons Magic had been a Laker, they made the playoffs. And for the third time in his career, Magic was voted the Most Valuable Player of the NBA.

But for only the third time in Magic's eleven years with the Lakers, Los Angeles didn't make it as far as the NBA finals. The Phoenix Suns ousted Los Angeles in the Western Conference finals even though Magic had an impressive series, scoring 43 points apiece in Game 4 and Game 5 of the series and tying an NBA record for assists in a playoff game with 24.

When Kareem Abdul-Jabbar retired after twenty seasons in the NBA, Magic was asked if he thought he would last that long in the league. He answered that he didn't think *anyone* else would play as long as Jabbar had. It was taking longer for his bruises to heal, and there were other things that Magic wanted to do in life.

Magic was aware that many athletes didn't prepare for their life after their athletic careers were over. "When the crowds quit cheering, they forget you fast. You have to plan. I have."

As a superstar in the NBA, Magic was asked to endorse products and make commercials for several companies. Over the years, Magic had done that for Converse, Disneyland, Kentucky Fried Chicken, and Nestle Crunch. By the early 1990's, Magic was earning $9 million a year in commercial endorsements. That was about three times what he was earning as a professional basketball player.

In 1987, Magic's contract with the Los Angeles Lakers was rewritten. Instead of the $1 million a year for 25 years that was settled on in 1981, Magic now received more than $2 million a year to play for the Lakers.

It wasn't the money, though, that drove Magic toward his dream of being a successful businessman. He wanted young African Americans to see that they had opportunities other than sports to be successful in life.

"I was given the gifts to become not only an athlete but also a businessman, a thinker, who could dispel the myth that most athletes are just dumb jocks. My business success has helped so many young blacks to learn that they, if they play ball, can be both athletes and businessmen."

Magic owns a T-shirt company called Magic Johnson T's. He also owns three stores in the

Los Angeles area named Magic's 32, after his Laker number, that sell sports clothing, shoes, and accessories. Nintendo markets an electronic video game called "Magic Johnson's Fast Break," designed after the Laker's running "Showtime" offense.

The business that Magic is most interested in is a part ownership he has in a Pepsi Cola bottling company in Washington, DC. In June of 1990, Magic invested more than $15 million to become part owner of the soft drink factory.

If his business partners and the workers in the bottling plant thought Magic was just lending his name and his money to the business, they were wrong. Like everything else he did, Magic put a great deal of effort into his new business venture.

Magic was often in Washington for days at a time looking after every aspect of the business. In basketball, it's passing, rebounding, and shooting. In business, it's profits, losses, and executive meetings. In basketball he is Magic. In business he is Earvin. Or Mr. Johnson.

With his name and title — executive vice president — on his office door at Pepsi, Earvin Johnson, Jr., is often reminded of those Friday nights cleaning offices and dreaming of one day being the boss. "Now I am," he says with a smile.

For several summers, Magic has also run basketball camps in Detroit, San Diego, and Los Angeles. If the kids show up thinking they are in for a two-week vacation with an NBA superstar, they are sadly mistaken. Magic makes it clear on the first day that camp is not going to be all fast breaks, high fives, and a one-man Magic show.

"Don't waste your time here because it's gonna be all work. We'll get to the gym early and we'll stay late," Magic lectures the young hopefuls. "You're gonna be tired, hungry, and you might even miss your mom, but if you want to learn to play basketball, this is the place to be."

Basketball is just what they learn — Magic's way. They learn through hours and hours of passing, dribbling, and shooting as well as through defensive drills. Magic stresses what all of his coaches taught him. The three keys to victory are defense, defense, and defense.

The kids work hard and, when they think they can't do anything else, Magic tells them that Larry Bird takes almost 1,000 shots in an empty gym before each game. Or that Michael Jordan practices his moves over and over again so that, when he is in a game, he can more easily maneuver himself past an unsuspecting opponent.

When the sessions end, the kids are always sorry to leave. Besides learning more than they ever thought they would about basketball, the kids have seen the rewards of hard work.

No matter what time they show up at the gym in the morning, Magic is already there. And he would be there — still taking shots, still practicing rebounding and dribbling — long after the campers had called it a day. Magic had learned that lesson from his father. And now it was his turn to teach that lesson to anyone who would listen.

At the end of the 1989–90 season, Laker coach Pat Riley retired and became a broadcaster with NBC Sports. Mike Dunleavy replaced Riley, but he didn't replace the Laker's fast-paced style of "Showtime" basketball.

During the 1990–91 season Magic broke the NBA record for career assists, held by Oscar Robertson. Because he was proud of the way both he and Larry Bird had elevated the passing game to an art form, this was a record that meant a lot to Magic. "It is something that pays tribute to all the great passers who came before me," Magic said when he broke the record.

The 1990–91 season also began what many fans saw as a new rivalry between two superstars when Magic and the Lakers met Michael Jordan and the Bulls in the NBA finals.

As Magic and Larry Bird ended their twelfth seasons in the NBA, many fans of the game saw Michael Jordan as the next superstar. Magic agreed. Especially after Chicago whipped the Lakers to win the NBA championship four games to one.

Magic understood what winning the championship meant to any player — but especially to such a talented competitor as Michael Jordan. Magic had experienced a championship during his rookie season in 1979–80. But the Bulls hadn't won a title in Jordan's first five years and fans were beginning to think Jordan didn't have what it took to lead his team to the title.

So when Jordan and the Bulls won the title, one player understood better than most. "I've heard so much talk about him as an individual player, but he's proved everyone wrong with this championship. It's going to taste sweet. There's no better feeling," said Magic after the final game.

During the summer of 1991, Magic worked at Pepsi, ran his summer camps, and hosted another "A Midsummer Night's Magic" benefit.

Then on September 14, 1991, Magic got married. He married Earletha Kelly, better known as Cookie. The wedding was held in East Lansing. Magic's best man was Isiah Thomas of the Detroit Pistons.

Just before his wedding, Magic and his agent began to talk with the Lakers about a way to raise Magic's salary. Magic was to make $2.5 million for the 1991–92 season and that did not even put him close in earnings to Larry Bird's estimated $7 million in salary and bonuses with the Boston Celtics.

The NBA limits the payrolls of NBA teams. This means that a team cannot just go out and pay their players as much as they want. After the Lakers signed Sam Perkins, the team had reached their salary limit and they could not pay Magic more money. Laker owner, Jerry Buss, felt his star player deserved more money, so he decided to give Magic a $3-million loan.

In a situation such as this (where so much money is being invested), it is common for an NBA team to take out an insurance policy on their player. And insurance companies make the player take a physical examination to make certain of his health.

Meanwhile, the Lakers went to France to play some exhibition games in Paris. Upon returning to Los Angeles, Magic felt a little tired. He felt, as did his doctors, that it was from the thirteen-hour return flight from Paris to Los Angeles.

The new season was approaching and Magic played in a couple of preseason games on October 22 and October 23.

On October 25, 1991, Magic was in his hotel room in Salt Lake City, Utah, resting before a preseason game with the Jazz, when the phone rang. It was the team doctor in Los Angeles.

10
Magic's New Life

Dr. Michael Mellman, the Los Angeles Lakers' team physician, told Magic to return to Los Angeles immediately. Now it was Magic's turn to use his imagination. He couldn't understand why Dr. Mellman wanted him to report to his office so quickly. He got on a plane and returned to Los Angeles.

"Earvin, sit down, I have some test results," the doctor said. "You're HIV positive."

Immediately, Magic thought he had AIDS. "Like almost everyone else who had not paid attention to the growing AIDS epidemic in the U.S. and the rest of the world, I didn't know the difference between the virus and the disease."

Magic's first thoughts were about his wife, Cookie. The newlyweds had just found out that Cookie was pregnant. Cookie and the unborn baby would also have to be tested.

Magic also went through more testing to make sure the insurance company's doctor hadn't made a mistake. Less than two weeks later, Dr. Mellman and another of Magic's doctors, Dr. David Ho, went to Magic's house and told him, while Cookie sat beside him, that he was indeed HIV positive.

During those two weeks, Cookie and their unborn baby had been tested. Both tested negative, which meant that neither had the virus.

In the days after finding out he was HIV positive, Magic began to learn all he could about HIV and AIDS. Magic found out that being HIV positive is not the same as having AIDS. HIV is the virus that causes AIDS. At the same time, Magic found out that he would most likely contract AIDS within the next ten years.

But in the meantime, there were medicines that would help his immune system, the part of the body that HIV attacks. Those medicines could help keep Magic healthy and allow him to live a fairly normal life.

Would a normal life include continuing to play in the NBA? His doctors said no. Because of the physical demands of the game, the lack of sleep due to extensive traveling, and the long NBA season, Magic's doctors told him it would be best to retire. The constant physical nature of professional basketball could easily weaken Magic's immune system and allow the virus to grow stronger more quickly. Magic's doctors felt playing pro basketball was too much of a risk to his immune system, and Magic sadly agreed.

It was perhaps his toughest decision. But once Magic decided to retire, he turned the void into his next challenge. He would face it as he had faced his knee injury in his second season and his sister Mary's death from leukemia in 1987. "OK, that's it," Magic said. "I'll deal with it."

Magic also decided to become a spokesman for HIV and AIDS education. Reading about the epidemic, Magic learned that more than half of Americans who were HIV positive or had AIDS were African-American or Hispanic. He was determined not to let Americans, especially young Americans, think that AIDS was somebody else's disease. Magic was going to spread the word that anyone could get infected with the virus. After all, he had.

In the meantime though, Magic had to tell his teammates, his close friends, and finally, the world that he was HIV positive. On the night his two doctors confirmed that he was HIV positive, Magic decided it was time to go public. The next afternoon, Magic delivered the news that stunned the world.

On November 7, 1991, Coach Mike Dunleavy of the Lakers called a team meeting for 2 P.M. Since leaving the team in Salt Lake City on October 25, the official word had been that Magic was suffering from the flu. But his teammates and Laker fans were beginning to wonder. The NBA season had started and Magic had missed the first three games.

Before Magic showed up at the Forum to talk to his fellow Lakers, he called some of his closest friends. He had already called his parents in East Lansing. They knew. But there were other people that Magic wanted to tell before he told the world.

One of the people Magic called was his ten-year-old son Andre. Magic and Andre's mother never married, but Magic was close to his son and wanted to assure him that he still loved him.

Magic also called his closest friends in the NBA: Larry Bird, Michael Jordan, and Isiah Thomas. Michael Jordan was in his car when Magic reached him on his phone. "I'm almost driving off the road because I couldn't handle it as well as he could," Jordan said the day after Magic's call. "I told him that I loved him and my family's with him and whatever we can do, we're willing to do that."

Magic also called his good friend Arsenio Hall, who hosts a nationwide TV talk show out of Los Angeles. When Magic asked if he could go on Hall's show the next night, the talk show host immediately said yes.

Magic also called Pat Riley, his former coach, who had returned to coaching and was preparing the New York Knicks for a game against the Orlando Magic. Riley was only able to listen in stunned silence.

Finally it was time to enter the Laker locker room and deliver the news to his teammates. Magic was smiling when he entered the locker room. Like he had smiled everyday for the past twelve seasons.

But as he told the Lakers he was HIV positive, and was retiring from pro basketball, Magic started to cry for the first time since October 25. Soon all the Lakers were in tears. The tears didn't last for long. Magic told his teammates that being HIV positive was just another challenge. A challenge like playing the Celtics in the Garden. Then Magic went out and told the world he was HIV positive. And that he was going to become a spokesman for HIV and AIDS.

Magic began to spread the word the next night. He appeared on the Arsenio Hall show. The message Magic began to spread was that being HIV positive was not the same as having AIDS. And that he should not be treated any different just because he was HIV positive. "I'll still be the same happy-go-lucky guy I've always been, not someone you should be afraid of."

A few days later, President Bush asked Magic to become a member of the National Commission on AIDS, a federal agency that studies the virus. The commission makes recommendations to the government on what it can do to help fight the spread of AIDS.

When Magic first announced that he was HIV positive, he didn't say how he had gotten the virus that causes AIDS. The week after making his announcement, Magic wrote an article for *Sports Illustrated*. He said that he had gotten the virus from having unprotected sex with a woman. Before he married Cookie, Magic had been a bachelor. As a bachelor, Magic had many girlfriends. He was telling the world that he hadn't used protection because he had thought HIV and AIDS were diseases that affected other people. He now realized that anyone could get the virus and develop AIDS. *Anyone.*

In early December, Magic did an interview on national television with Connie Chung of CBS News. "You can't really get it from kissing, touching, feeling. You can't. It really doesn't happen that way," Magic said. He also wanted to make an important point because, he admitted, "Even I had not been listening."

"What I am trying to do," Magic told Connie Chung, "is educate the heterosexuals. They need to be educated. Now AIDS itself, yes, we've been prone to think, OK, it's through homosexual activity, and yes, a lot of that's happened. But, with this virus, 75 percent of the people who have it worldwide are heterosexual. That's why the public has got to be educated about this."

And Magic felt he could help with educating the public. In his interview with Connie Chung, he said, "This is not a one-person disease. This is an everybody disease. So, I don't care how you get it. I'm here to help you."

Magic began to give lectures about safer sex.

He talked to kids, he went to Washington, DC, to join the AIDS Commission, and he talked to President Bush.

Some people thought that Magic might be giving the wrong message because he was telling young people to use condoms when having sex. Isn't no sex, the safest sex, asked many people?

"The safest sex is no sex," responded Magic. And he meant it. But he also realized that some teenagers will have sex, no matter what their parents and teachers tell them about AIDS and other sexually transmitted diseases. It is those teenagers he wants to reach.

With Magic leading the way, there was no possibility that anyone would be able to ignore HIV and AIDS. Besides his message of safer sex, Magic had another message to send out to Americans about people who were HIV positive. "I'm still the same Magic," he said on Arsenio Hall's talk show. "When you see me coming, you can still give me the same hugs, the same high fives, the kisses."

In February, 1992, Magic proved yet one more point. Just because he was HIV positive did not mean his life was over or that he could not play basketball. And for one afternoon, the Magic was back on the basketball court.

11
The Magic Lives On

When the ballots were counted for the 1992 NBA All-Star Game, Magic Johnson had been voted to start for the Western All-Stars. Even though he had retired from playing basketball, he was still a fan favorite.

Immediately, Magic knew he wanted to play in the game. And his doctors told him he was healthy enough to play. However, some people thought that Magic might give the virus to the other players during the game.

Dr. William M. Reiter, an expert on AIDS and HIV, told *The New York Times*, "There is so much ignorance about how you get it; there is such a lack of education. There is probably a greater risk of someone getting killed in a car accident on the way to the basketball game than getting the AIDS virus from another player in the game itself."

Charles Barkley, from the Philadelphia 76ers, a starter for the Eastern All-Stars, looked forward to playing against Magic. "I'm going to play Magic the same way I play against anybody else: to win. I'm not afraid. Why should I be afraid?"

Before the game, Magic said, "I wouldn't put myself at risk, nor would I put anyone else in a life-threatening situation." Magic was determined to educate people. "I have to be out there for myself and I have to be out there for a lot of people, whether they have a disease or whether they have a handicap. And let them see they can carry on, and still live, and don't have to feel that they are different."

The game was held in Orlando on February 9, 1992. More than 14,000 fans jammed the Orlando Arena to watch Magic and the rest of the All-Stars play in the 42nd annual NBA All-Star Game. Millions more watched the game on television.

From the beginning, it was an emotional afternoon for Magic, the other players, and the fans. The Eastern All-Stars were introduced. The fans cheered for Charles Barkley, Patrick Ewing, Michael Jordan, Isiah Thomas, Scott Pippen, and the rest of the stars from the Eastern Conference. Then it was time for the Western All-Stars to be introduced. First the reserve players were called on to the court, one by one. Then the starting five were introduced: Karl Malone of the Utah Jazz, Chris Mullen of the Golden State Warriors, David Robinson of the San Antonio Spurs, and Clyde Drexler of the Portland Trailblazers. The fans cheered each star.

Then, it was time for Magic.

"And starting at the other guard," began the announcer, "the NBA's all-time leader in assists. . . ." The rest of the introduction could barely be heard as the crowd rose to its feet and began to cheer for Magic. Their hero was back where he belonged. On the basketball court.

For two minutes, the crowd continued to cheer. A sign went up, THE MAGIC IS BACK. And as the crowd continued to cheer for Magic, something wonderful happened. Magic's good friend, Isiah Thomas, the captain of the Eastern All-Stars, slowly walked over to him. He kissed his friend, put his arms around him, and gave Magic a big hug. Then, one by one, each player from the Eastern All-Stars walked up to Magic and hugged him. It was an emotional show of support for Magic.

Finally it was time for the game. And in no time, it was obvious that Magic was back — just like before. Early in the first quarter, Karl Malone pulled down a defensive rebound. He passed the ball to Magic who threw one of his famous halfcourt passes to Clyde Drexler who then passed it to Chris Mullen. Mullen made a basket before the Eastern All-Stars were even down court. The crowd roared. It was "Showtime" in Orlando.

Throughout the game, Magic proved that he could still play basketball with the best. He was all over the court, driving the lane to make a lay-up, passing the ball behind his back to a teammate coming down court, and leading the Western All-Stars to a 153–113 victory over the Eastern All-Stars.

Even though the game became one sided, nobody left the Orlando Arena before it was over. As it turned out, Magic saved the best for last. In the final minutes, Magic put on a show. He took two outside shots that went through the basket for three points each. The crowd loved it.

Then he proved the point that he always taught in his basketball camps: The key to victory is defense. As Isiah Thomas brought the ball toward the basket, Magic came out and challenged his friend to score against him. Isiah did some fancy dribbling; he faked to his right, dribbled some more, then faked to his left. Magic stayed right with him. As the shot clock ran out, Isiah drove to the basket, but Magic was on him. Isiah was forced to take a shot from outside that missed. The crowd cheered Magic's defensive abilities.

Next it was Michael Jordan's turn. After Isiah missed his shot, the West grabbed the rebound and quickly scored a basket. As Jordan brought the ball back up court toward the basket, Magic came out to challenge the Chicago Bulls' superstar to score against him. The crowd rose to its feet and cheered its approval.

Jordan faked left and then drove toward the basket to his right. As Jordan lifted himself off the floor for the jump shot, Magic put his right arm up to block it. The ball went over Magic's outstretched hand but it did not go in the basket. Again the crowd roared.

With just seconds left in the game, Magic brought the ball down court one last time. He gave the crowd a smile as he dribbled toward the basket. And the crowd just cheered and cheered. With just fifteen seconds left in the game, Magic took one last shot. It was a three-point attempt from 25 feet out. The ball went through the basket without even touching the rim. And that ended the ball game.

All the players crowded around Magic and hugged him. Even though there were about 14 seconds left in the game, the action on the court just stopped. Someone said it was the first game called on account of hugs.

Magic had proven his point. He finished the game with 25 points, 9 assists, and 5 rebounds, and was voted the Most Valuable Player of the All-Star Game.

In accepting the MVP award, Magic smiled and spoke to the crowd in the Orlando Arena. "First of all," began Magic, "let me thank the fans who voted me here. Without them I wouldn't be here." The crowd roared its approval. "I'd also like to thank the players who decided it would be all right to play with me and against me." Again the crowd roared.

Then Magic turned his attention to a special woman sitting in the Arena. "I'd like to thank my wife for putting up with me for the last three or four months. It's been tough on her and she deserves a lot of credit. Cookie, I love you."

Magic ended his speech by telling the crowd, "Maybe you will see me back and maybe you won't, but I will always remember all of these good times this afternoon and I'd like to thank you for sharing this with me. Thank you."

It had been a special afternoon for basketball. But would Magic ever play again? He is planning on going to Barcelona to play in the Olympics but, after the All-Star Game, nobody knew if he would play another NBA game.

For Magic, there was more to think about than basketball. He was going to continue to spread his message of living with HIV. It seemed there was no better spokesperson than Magic.

"God must have known what he was doing when he chose me. He knew that my outlook on life wouldn't change. He knew that I would continue to stay strong and not really worry about what people would say and what their opinion was about me. The good and the bad was going to come with it. I was still going to stay myself," Magic said in a television interview before the All-Star Game.

Magic also summed up how he felt about living with HIV. "Life doesn't stop because something dramatic happens to you. I'm not going to let it stop me. I'm going to continue on. It's the only way I know how. I've got to keep on fighting, keep on smiling, and keep on having a good time. I'll be all right. Here I am, still Earvin Johnson, Jr."

At the end of the interview, Earvin "Magic" Johnson, Jr., had one more thing to say to America. Only this time he didn't say it with words. He said it with his smile. It was, as always, the smile of a true American champion.

More About Magic

Career Highlights

Magic enjoyed an incredible twelve seasons with the Los Angeles Lakers. His highlights include the following:
- NBA Most Valuable Player (MVP) in 1987, 1989, and 1990.
- Nine-time member of All-NBA First Team, 1983–1991
- Playoff MVP in 1980, 1982, 1987
- All-Star Game MVP in 1992
- Member of five NBA championship teams in 1980, 1982, 1985, 1987, and 1988
- Career NBA assist leader (9,921)
- NBA assist leader in 1983 (829), 1984 (875), 1986 (907), and 1987 (977)
- NBA leader in steals in 1982 (208)
- NBA free-throw percentage leader in 1989 (.911)

• Holds career NBA playoff record for most assists (2,320)
• Shares NBA playoff-game record for most assists (24) in 1984
• Career leader in All-Star Game assists (118)
• Holds record for most assists in All-Star Game (22) in 1984

Books

Guttman, Bill. *Magic: More Than a Legend*. New York: Harper Paperbacks, 1992.

Johnson, Earvin, Jr., and Roy S. Johnson. *Magic's Touch*. Reading, MA: Addison-Wesley, 1989.

Levin, Richard. *Magic Johnson: Court Magician*. Chicago: Children's Press, 1981.

Lovitt, Chip. *Magic Johnson*. New York: Scholastic, 1991.

Pascarelli, Peter F. *The Courage of Magic Johnson*. New York: Bantam Books, 1991.

Videos

Back-to-Back: The Lakers Season, 1987–88. CBS Fox Video, 1988.

Final Four, The Movie. JCI Video, Inc., 1988.

Magic Johnson: Put Magic in Your Game. CBS Fox Video, 1989.

More Information About AIDS and HIV

The National AIDS Hotline: 1-800-342-AIDS
Teens Teaching AIDS Prevention: 1-800-234-
   TEEN

About the Author

BILL MORGAN is a free-lance writer living in New York City. Bill has written books on Miami Dolphin quarterback Dan Marino and San Antonio Spur center David Robinson. Currently Bill is writing books for Scholastic on Roger Clemens, Bobby Bonilla, and Barry Sanders.

SCHOLASTIC BIOGRAPHY

☐ MP44075-6	Bo Jackson: Playing the Games	$2.95
☐ MP42396-7	Christopher Columbus: Admiral of the Ocean Sea	$2.95
☐ MP45243-6	Colin Powell: A Biography	$2.95
☐ MP41836-X	Custer and Crazy Horse: A Story of Two Warriors	$2.95
☐ MP44570-7	The Death of Lincoln: A Picture History of the Assassination	$2.95
☐ MP45225-8	The Fairy Tale Life of Hans Christian Andersen	$2.75
☐ MP42218-9	Frederick Douglass Fights for Freedom	$2.50
☐ MP43628-7	Freedom Train: The Story of Harriet Tubman	$2.95
☐ MP43730-5	George Washington: The Man Who Would Not Be King	$2.75
☐ MP42402-5	Harry Houdini: Master of Magic	$2.50
☐ MP42404-1	Helen Keller	$2.50
☐ MP44652-5	Helen Keller's Teacher	$2.95
☐ MP44230-9	I Have a Dream: The Story of Martin Luther King	$2.75
☐ MP44336-4	Jennifer Capriati	$2.95
☐ MP42395-9	Jesse Jackson: A Biography	$2.75
☐ MP43503-5	Jim Abbott: Against All Odds	$2.75
☐ MP41344-9	John Fitzgerald Kennedy: America's 35th President	$2.50
☐ MP43827-1	The Life and Words of Martin Luther King, Jr.	$2.75
☐ MP41159-4	Lost Star: The Story of Amelia Earhart	$2.75
☐ MP44350-X	Louis Braille: The Boy Who Invented Books for the Blind	$2.75
☐ MP44154-X	Nelson Mandela "No Easy Walk to Freedom"	$2.95
☐ MP44144-2	New Kids in Town: Oral Histories of Immigrant Teens	$2.95
☐ MP42644-3	Our 41st President George Bush	$2.95
☐ MP43481-0	Pocahontas and the Strangers	$2.95
☐ MP41877-7	Ready, Aim, Fire! The Real Life Adventures of Annie Oakley	$2.75
☐ MP43052-1	The Secret Soldier: The Story of Deborah Sampson	$2.75
☐ MP44055-1	Squanto, Friend of the Pilgrims	$2.75
☐ MP42560-9	Stealing Home: The Story of Jackie Robinson	$2.95
☐ MP42660-5	The Story of George Washington Carver	$2.95
☐ MP42403-3	The Story of Thomas Alva Edison	$2.75
☐ MP45605-9	This Is David Robinson	$2.95
☐ MP42904-3	The Wright Brothers at Kitty Hawk	$2.95

Available wherever you buy books, or use this order form.

Scholastic Inc., P.O. Box 7502, 2931 East McCarty Street, Jefferson City, MO 65102

Please send me the books I have checked above. I am enclosing $_____ (please add $2.00 to cover shipping and handling). Send check or money order — no cash or C.O.D.s please.

Name _____

Address _____

City _____ State/Zip _____

Please allow four to six weeks for delivery. Available in the U.S. only. Sorry, mail orders are not available to residents of Canada. Prices subject to change.   BIO792